THE LATE VICTORIANS
A SHORT HISTORY

HERMAN AUSUBEL
Columbia University

AN ANVIL ORIGINAL
under the general editorship of
LOUIS L. SNYDER

D. VAN NOSTRAND COMPANY, INC.

TORONTO   LONDON

To

Rebecca and Harry

VAN NOSTRAND REGIONAL OFFICES:
New York, Chicago, San Francisco

D. VAN NOSTRAND COMPANY, LTD., *London*

D. VAN NOSTRAND COMPANY (Canada), LTD., *Toronto*

PREFACE

Most general accounts of the late Victorian period have been narrative histories—descriptions of the past with a minimum of interpretation. Nowadays such histories are out of fashion. The present generation of historians expects every historical study to have a thesis. Unless it drives home a central point, it is not worth publishing. Interpretative history is fun to write, but it is also hazardous to write, for it often tempts the historian to ignore or belittle data that does not fit his thesis and to oversimplify and distort his presentation. Fortunately, there are always other historians to point out these deficiencies and modify and even destroy the thesis. If, despite its dangers, interpretative history has a bright future, the main reason is simple. Present-day historians, like so many of their contemporaries, are eager for answers and explanations.

The present volume is an interpretative history of England in the last decades of the nineteenth century. It makes no effort to "cover" the age. Such an attempt would have converted a short book into a catalogue of names, dates, and events, and enough such chronicles already exist. Instead, it centers on the great depression from which the late Victorians suffered and the effects on their lives of what they called "hard times." It concentrates on this particular subject because Englishmen in the last decades of the nineteenth century considered it so overwhelmingly important.

The volume is based mainly on primary source materials—on what the late Victorians said and wrote about what they did and thought. The documents with which it concludes are designed to illustrate the main points made in the text. These documents have been drawn chiefly from sources that are not readily available.

The author hopes that this book may encourage the reader to appreciate the wisdom of Sir James Barrie's remark, made in a period when hostility to the Victorians was widespread, "Don't forget to speak scornfully of the Victorian age; there will be time for meekness when you try to better it."

HERMAN AUSUBEL

TABLE OF CONTENTS

PART I—THE LATE VICTORIAN AGE

1. Introduction   9
2. The Plight of Agriculture   12
3. Industrial and Commercial Depression   18
4. The Condition of the Working Classes   28
5. The State an Enemy   37
6. The State a Friend   47
7. Socialist Dissension   60
8. Irish Agitation   72
9. Clamor for Empire   81
10. Conclusion   89

PART II—DOCUMENTS FROM THE
LATE VICTORIAN PERIOD

1. The Royal Commission Reports on the Causes
   of Agricultural Depression, 1882   95
2. Another Royal Commission Discusses the
   Causes of Agricultural Depression, 1897   97
3. A Trade Union Song of Agricultural Workers   100
4. Joseph Arch on His Union of Farm Workers,
   1882   102
5. Agricultural Workers and the Depression, 1882 104
6. The Royal Commission Analyzes the Commercial and Industrial Depression, 1886   105
7. Joseph Arch on Free Trade and Protection,
   1884   108
8. E. E. Williams' *Made in Germany,* 1896   111
9. The Advantages of England's Rivals, 1897   113
10. Professor Levi on the Condition of the Working
    Classes, 1885   115
11. Sweated Workers, 1890   117
12. Trade Unionism: For and Against, 1894   122
13. The Doctrines of the Liberty and Property
    Defence League, 1885   126
14. The Menace of Socialism, 1890   130

15. W. H. Mallock and the Offensive of the Individualists, 1894   133
16. Disraeli and the Health of the People, 1872   135
17. Lord Randolph Churchill's Tory Democracy, 1883   139
18. Joseph Chamberlain: Scourge of the Individualists, 1885   143
19. William Morris Composes Socialist Chants, 1885   147
20. The Basis of the Fabian Society, 1887   151
21. Robert Blatchford's *Merrie England,* 1894   153
22. Socialists on the Royal Commission on Labour, 1894   157
23. Michael Davitt and the Land League, 1882   160
24. Liberal Converts to Home Rule   166
25. Matthew Arnold and Irish Anarchy, 1886   169
26. J. A. Froude on the Economics of Empire, 1886   172
27. Joseph Chamberlain and Imperial Coöperation, 1897   176
28. Tennyson as a Poet of Empire   179
    Select Bibliography   183
    Index   185

Part I

THE LATE VICTORIAN AGE

1

INTRODUCTION

The Great Depression.   In the last decades of the nineteenth century the English people suffered from a depression—worldwide in its incidence—that was of central importance in the shaping of their history. Scholars have rarely given sufficient attention to this depression and the great variety of its repercussions. Yet it clarifies much of the political, social, economic, and intellectual development of the late Victorians. It helps to explain what happened to their agriculture, industry, commerce, and the condition of their working classes. It throws much light on the history of their government and churches and their ideas about the rôle these institutions should play in their lives. And it helps to account for their relations with Ireland and their empire and their opinions about what those relations should be.

A Time of Troubles.   Present-day Englishmen often view the last decades of the nineteenth century as a golden age. Accustomed to depression, war, austerity, and fear of another war and another depression, they consider the late Victorians an extremely fortunate generation. Yet if Englishmen of the atomic era dug into the documents that their predecessors left in such profusion, they would quickly discover that their image of the past bears little relation to reality. They would find that the late Victorians did not consider their age stable and secure. Whether they belonged to the upper, middle, or lower classes, they thought of themselves as living in a time of troubles. They had complicated problems to solve, and they disagreed sharply as to how to go about solving them. Whatever else may be said of them—and much that is untrue and unfair has been said of them—self-complacency was not one of their characteristics. Some of them even concluded that because of the pressures and tensions of the time their countrymen were "falling more and more a prey to neurotic diseases." When in 1897 the Commissioners in Lunacy brought out a special report on the alleged increase of insanity, they started with the assumption that "the hurry and restless movement, the keen competition and struggle, the growth and corresponding evils of large cities" must necessarily have produced a rise in the incidence of mental illness.

A Changing Population.   Probably the most remarkable developments of the late Victorian age—and to some people of the time the most alarming—were the changes that took place in the size and distribution of the population. According to the census of 1871, there were almost 23 million people in England and Wales. Because of the decline of the death rate, which resulted from the growth and application of medical knowledge, this figure had increased thirty years later by 10 million—despite the emigration during the intervening period of more than 3½ million Englishmen to the United States, British North America, Australasia, and other places. This 10 million increase alone was almost three times the size of the population of Elizabethan England.

Not only did the population grow appreciably in late Victorian times, but its distribution was impressively altered. In 1871, the census returns classified three-fifths of the people as urban and two-fifths as rural. By the end of Victoria's reign in 1901 more than three-fourths were urban and less than one-fourth rural. In a sense these proportions are deceptive, for the census defined as urban any community with 2000 or more inhabitants, although such a community was often little more than an overgrown village. Even when allowance is made for this inadequacy of the statistics, the figures remain eloquent.

Deserted Villages.   Farsighted Victorians viewed as ominous these changes in the size and distribution of the population. On the one hand, some of them joined neo-Malthusian groups, whose purpose it was to spread knowledge of methods of birth control, especially among the poorer elements in society. In this way they hoped to reduce the tensions in a period of economic distress. On the other hand, propagandists emerged to resist the growing urbanization of English society, insisting that it meant the progressive deterioration of the race and, therefore, national disaster. They defended agriculture not only as an occupation but as a living art, a mother of men, and a way of life, and they lamented the fact that in an age of depression people were rejecting the villages where their forefathers had lived for generations. In the future the armed forces would have to come from towns, and the publicists had great doubts that such sailors and soldiers would have either the patriotism or the physical stamina of their country-bred predecessors. Town dwellers, said a spokesman for rural England, have developed a "flaccidity and decrepitude which proclaim that hardness, grit, and that unbending temper and unyielding courage, which are among the most distinguishing traits of the Anglo-Saxon race, are disappearing." Another agricultural spokesman cautioned his countrymen that "upon the well-being of Great Britain's oldest industry [agriculture] depend the ultimate economic welfare of her people, their physical and mental virility, and that healthy outlook upon national problems which alone can maintain her pre-eminent position among the nations of the world." The publicists were rarely hopeful that they would halt, much less reverse, the exodus from the countryside; nor did they. Parts of rural England, many travelers remarked, became as deserted as the veld of Africa.

2

THE PLIGHT OF AGRICULTURE

Farming a Grim Business. Landlords, tenant farmers, and laborers found agriculture a grim business in the late Victorian period. They were plagued by a depression that began in the mid-seventies, and while it varied in severity, it lasted almost until the end of the nineteenth century. Searching for explanations of the hard times from which they suffered, they blamed each other, inclement weather, high taxes, the railroads, faulty techniques, the high cost of production, and the backward state of coöperative societies. Only gradually did they come to stress the cause that economists of a later generation have emphasized above all: foreign competition so acute that it far exceeded the anticipations both of those who favored and opposed the repeal of the Corn Laws and the coming of freer trade back in the 1840's. With the expansion of agricultural production especially in the United States, the improvement of foreign railroad and steamship facilities, and the lowering of costs of transportation, the English farming community ceased to enjoy the advantages—in particular "the natural protection of distance"—it had had in the past. Royal commissions of investigation and inquiry were appointed to diagnose the maladies of rural England and to recommend remedies. (*See Documents No. 1 and 2.*) Many books and pamphlets—*The British Farmer and His Competitors* (1888), *The Truth about Agricultural Depression* (1897), and *The Ruin of Rural England: A Warning* (1901) are the titles of a few of them—were written to suggest ways to overcome the distress of the countryside. Indeed, the depression helps to account for the tremendous popularity that the American land reformer, Henry George, and his ideas on *Progress and Poverty* (1879) enjoyed in late Victorian England.

Farmers in other European countries were also threatened by the invasion of American prairie wheat and other products, but they appealed successfully to their governments for assistance. In the France of the Third Republic and in Bismarckian Germany, tariffs were adopted to protect domestic agriculture from foreign competition. Despite similar appeals from the farming community in England, no such policy was pursued. For two reasons this might seem surprising. First, the Conservative Party held office frequently in the late Victorian period, and many of its members viewed themselves preëminently as spokesmen for the agricultural interest. In fact, Disraeli's great ministry (1874-1880) coincided with the early years of the depression. Secondly, there had been a number of European wars in the years before the coming of hard times: the Austro-Sardinian War (1859), the Danish War (1864), the Austro-Prussian War (1866), and the Franco-German War (1870-1871). If, therefore, domestic agriculture was ruined by foreign competition and the country became increasingly dependent on American and other sources of food supply, what would happen should England take part in a European conflict? As a popular journalist put it: "But don't you see, Mr. Smith, that if we lose our power to feed ourselves *we destroy the advantages of our insular position?* Don't you see that if we destroy our agriculture we destroy our independence at a blow, and become a defenseless nation? Don't you see that the people who depend on foreigners for their food are at the mercy of any ambitious statesman who chooses to make war upon them? And don't you think that is a rather stiff price to pay to get a farthing off the loaf?" Furthermore, the fear was often expressed that Britain's involvement in war would be followed not only by national starvation but by a revolution at home and the dissolution of the Empire. The threat of starvation, as events were to prove, was no mere specter of the alarmist.

State Help.   Successive governments did give some aid to the agricultural community, though spokesmen for rural England often complained that the clamor of urban groups had for decades been occupying "the whole attention of Parliament." Steps were taken to provide tax relief, to combat disease among livestock, to afford protection against the adulteration of farm fertilizers, seeds, and feed, to lower railroad rates, to encourage the improvement of land, and to keep farmers informed, through the establishment of a Board of Agriculture (1889), of the latest scientific discoveries and other useful information. The rural community became so accustomed to state intervention in its behalf during the last decades of the nineteenth century that, by the eve of World War I, a thoughtful writer on English agriculture could dedicate a book to a farmer friend whom he singled out because he was "one of the last defenders of the old *laissez-faire* position, a latter-day Athanasius, standing for self-help and honest individual work, and denouncing Government Departments, County Councils, Development Commissions, and all such spoon-feeding agencies."

If a protective tariff was out of the question, the reason was above all that no Parliament would dare to vote for such a measure. The towns were far more important in the House of Commons than the rural areas, and urban preponderance meant political ruin for the borough politician who favored a protective tariff and the higher food prices—the "dear loaf"—it would bring. In the well-chosen words of H. Rider Haggard, the author of *King Solomon's Mines,* who temporarily abandoned novel-writing in order to survey conditions in agricultural England: "The statesmen are few who, with the true interest of their Country at heart, would dare to risk the wrath of the inhabitants of towns, from whom they might suffer at the next election, by attempting acts of justice to the land whereof these did not approve." Protection in particular was a wretched word—"a piece of folly of which sensible men should be ashamed," as one ardent free trader phrased it. It had too many ugly associations with the hungry 1840's, when "people walked the streets like gaunt shadows, and not like human beings." Sir Walter Besant, the late Victorian novelist and reformer, argued that the cheap loaf was dearly bought if it rid the "countryside of its village folk, strong and healthy, and the empire of its stalwart soldiers," but most of his compatriots did not share his view.

The Struggle for Survival. In order to survive, landowners and farmers had to help themselves; they could not count on the kind of government aid the French and Germans were receiving. What often delayed their adaptation to the new conditions was the expectation that prosperity was just around the corner; hence many of them made few changes in their system of production. As it became clear that prosperity was not returning, they were forced to find ways to adjust to falling prices and foreign competition. Some economized by calling a halt to building and draining and by cutting down on the use of fertilizer. Some made more use of machinery in order to reduce production costs. Some shifted from the raising of wheat to the breeding and fattening of cattle and sheep. Some changed their methods of rotation. Some turned to breeding pedigreed stock, dairying, raising poultry, and growing flowers, fruits, and vegetables. Even for efficient and imaginative farmers and landowners it was a difficult era; for those who lacked flexibility it was an age of disaster. In the history of the decline of the English landed aristocracy the importance of the period of the great depression can hardly be exaggerated. Late Victorian audiences knew what Oscar Wilde meant in *The Importance of Being Earnest* (1895) when, after having one character in the play complain about being bored in the country, he had another add: "Ah! This is what the newspapers call agricultural depression, is it not? I believe the aristocracy are suffering very much from it just at present. It is almost an epidemic amongst them, I have been told."

The Fate of Farm Workers. As for the agricultural workers, their fate has been much disputed. The Royal Commission on Agriculture reported in 1882 that "the labouring class has been scarcely, if at all, affected by the distress which has fallen so heavily upon owners as well as occupiers." Few agricultural workers would have agreed, however, with the findings of the Commission. Many left for the industrial towns or encouraged their children to do so, for there they hoped to find higher wages and greater opportunities as well as amusement and excitement. "You're going to get on in the world, if I have any say in it, and leave working the land to them as can't do better for themselves," so ran the advice of parent after parent. Those who stayed on the farm either because of inertia, fear of change, or love of the soil had relatively little to look forward to. In a society that placed much stress on material success and getting ahead, they were widely viewed as failures. It was a sign of the times that Thomas Hardy, worrying about the illustrations that were to accompany *Far from the Madding Crowd* (1874), urged his publisher to be sure that "the rustics, although *quaint,* may be made to appear intelligent, and not boorish at all."

Attempts were made to raise the wages, limit the hours of work, and improve the social and political position of agricultural laborers through the establishment of a number of unions. (*See Document No. 3.*) Joseph Arch led the most important of these organizations, the National Agricultural Labourers' Union, which was founded on the eve of the agricultural depression. Arch's popularity among farm hands depended on his oratorical gifts and his reputation for standing up to people of rank and defending what he considered the rights of his class. Arch wanted laborers to have a chance to rise. He wanted them to be in a position to look with confidence to the future. He was convinced, he told the Royal Commission on Agriculture in 1881, that "if the farmers get well-fed labourers in good cottages with wholesome sleeping rooms, and with plenty to eat, they will get more profit out of their labour." His conception of how union members should behave is best stated in his own words: "Let courtesy, fairness and firmness characterise all our demands. Act cautiously and advisedly that no act have to be repented or repudiated. Do not strike unless all other means fail you. Try all other means; try them with firmness and patience. Try them only in the enforcement of just claims, and if they all fail, then strike." (*See Document No. 4.*) Other leaders of farm workers placed more emphasis on programs for the conversion of laborers into owners of small holdings.

Arch was eventually elected to Parliament, but his Union, though it achieved some successes, especially in encouraging emigration, was a depression casualty. Farmers by and large resisted workers' combinations. Their attitude was expressed in a union song of the 1870's:

> Says the master to me, "Is it true? I am told
> Your name on the books of the Union's enroll'd;
> I can never allow that a workman of mine,
> With wicked disturbers of peace should combine.

"I give you fair warning, mind what you're about,
Ï shall put my foot on it and trample it out;
On which side your bread's buttered, now sure you
    can see,
So decide now at once for the Union or me."

Worried about falling prices, farmers opposed organizations that sought to raise their expenditures on wages. Like their counterparts of an earlier time described in Samuel Butler's *The Way of All Flesh*, they were people who had "a sense of wrong that the weather was not more completely under their control, who desired higher prices and cheaper wages, but otherwise were most contented when things were changing least." They bemoaned the passing of the time when, as Walter Bagehot had noted in his masterpiece on *The English Constitution* (1867), peasants would pelt the agitator who tried to arouse dissatisfaction in the countryside. Farmers did not hesitate to use the lockout as a weapon in their struggle against unionism. In the words of another union song of the 1870's:

They have lock'd the farmers' labourers out,
    And many thousands now
In idleness must walk about
    Instead of being at the plough.

Farmers insisted that workers were better off than their fathers and grandfathers had been, and they were right. The enactment of several primary education laws starting in 1870 meant that the children of rural laborers had advantages unknown to their fathers; and when rural laborers received the right to vote in 1884 they had much greater opportunities to air their grievances. In strictly economic terms, they benefited by the dwindling supply of farm labor and by the falling prices of the great depression. Nevertheless, they pointed to their long hours of work, their few holidays, and the comparatively skilled character of their labor; and they complained that their wages, though better than in the past, were still distinctly below those of urban workers. They did not believe what they were often told—that they were doing better relatively than either landowners or farmers in the age of the great depression. (*See Document No. 5.*)

3

INDUSTRIAL AND COMMERCIAL DEPRESSION

Crisis in Industry and Commerce. Foreign competition and low prices made the late Victorian era a time of troubles for those engaged not only in agriculture but in industry and commerce as well. In the last decades of the nineteenth century English merchants and manufacturers became increasingly aware that they were losing their privileged position in the economic affairs of the world. They could testify to the accuracy of many of the predictions that had been set forth in an alarmist pamphlet of the 1850's entitled *The Darkening Cloud; or, England in Commercial Decline, and the Depression of Our National Industry from the Inroads of Foreign Competition.*

The Debate over the Depression. The depression from which English trade and industry suffered was, from a twentieth-century point of view, peculiar. Although the rate of increase of total industrial production fell off, labor-saving machinery and cost-cutting factories came more and more into their own, and output and real wages continued to mount impressively. While the direction of investment shifted from foreign to domestic channels and from high to low yield enterprises, the level of investment remained high. Many economists, therefore, have had misgivings about the use of the word depression to characterize the condition of the late nineteenth-century English economy. In a letter written in 1886 to the Royal Commission on the Depression of Trade and Industry, Professor Alfred Marshall, the eminent Cambridge economist, said: "It is doubtful whether the last 10 years, which are regarded as years of depression, but in which there have been few violent movements of prices, have not, on the whole, conduced more to solid progress and true happiness than the alternations of feverish activity and painful retrogression which have characterised every preceding decade of this century. In fact, I regard violent fluctuations of prices as a much greater evil than a gradual fall of prices." More recently such scholars as H. L. Beales and T. S. Ashton, of the London School of Economics, have also made it clear that they regard "the great depression" as an unfortunate label.

The fact remains that because commodity prices, profit margins, and interest rates fell almost continuously, late Victorian businessmen believed themselves doomed to struggle through lean years. They may have been wrong in their analysis, and economists may be right when they insist that the late Victorian economy was "consolidating and exploiting, on the whole, its previously opened resources rather than breaking new ground." But if the historian is to understand the past, he must try to think the way people of the past thought. And despite some brief upward turns and despite varying conditions in particular trades in different areas at different times, there is no doubt that the late Victorians considered theirs a period of business distress. The literature of economics that they produced—their speeches, books, pamphlets, journals, newspapers, and reports—swelled with complaints of hard times, falling prices and profits, and increasingly severe competition. Small wonder that late Victorian scholars came to pay more attention to the study of English economic history. Such classics as Thorold Rogers' *A History of Agriculture and Prices in England* and his *Six Centuries of Work and Wages,* William Cunningham's *Growth of English Industry and Commerce,* and Arnold Toynbee's *Industrial Revolution*—all reflect the influence of the great depression.

The time was past when the London *Times* could report, as it did in 1871: "We can . . . look on the present with undisturbed satisfaction. Our commerce is extending and multiplying its world-wide ramifications without much regard for the croaking of any political or scientific Cassandras. . . . Turn where we may, we find in our commerce no trace of decadence." The time had arrived when Lord Randolph Churchill, the Conservative politician who exploited the depression in many of his speeches, could proclaim (though with some exaggeration): "Your

iron industry is dead, dead as mutton; your coal industries, which depend greatly upon the iron industries, are
languishing. Your silk industry is dead, assassinated by
the foreigner. Your woollen industry is *in articulo mortis,*
gasping, struggling. Your cotton industry is seriously sick.
The shipbuilding industry, which held out longest of all,
is come to a standstill. Turn your eyes where you will,
survey any branch of British industry you like, you will
find signs of mortal disease." In these circumstances it is
not strange that harassed businessmen figured prominently among those who sought relief in the words and
music of Gilbert and Sullivan and in the escapist literature that was being written in late Victorian times by
Ouida, Marie Corelli, Robert Louis Stevenson, Sir Henry
Rider Haggard, Anthony Hope, and Sir Arthur Conan
Doyle.

In 1886 the Royal Commission which had been appointed to inquire into the depression of trade and industry completed its report. (*See Document No. 6.*)
Among the masses of evidence it accumulated concerning
the extent, nature, causes, and proposed cures of the
depression there appeared an "Analysis of Answers Received from Chambers of Commerce and Commercial
Associations." This valuable document makes it clear that
businessmen's organizations considered the causes of the
depression to be growing foreign competition, foreign
tariffs and bounties, overproduction, limitations on the
hours of labor, the influence of trade unions, the fall in
prices, credit inflation, the increase of taxation, the high
cost of transportation, agricultural distress, and pernicious
legislation. Among the remedial measures these organizations most often recommended were the removal or
modification of hostile tariffs and bounties, the formation
of a trading union between Britain and her colonies, the
more effective regulation of railway rates, the opening up
of new markets, the reorganization of the consular service, more emphasis on technical education, and tax
reform.

The late Victorian depression encouraged scores of
publicists to write for popular consumption about their
pet schemes. (*See Document No. 7.*) Pamphlets and
books appeared with these revealing titles:

Protection and Bad Times (1879)

Foreign Work and English Wages Considered with Reference to the Depression of Trade (1879)

England's Supremacy: Its Sources, Economics, and Dangers (1885)

The Trade Depression: Its Causes and Its Remedies (1885)

The Revival of British Industries: the Most Important Question at the Approaching General Election (1885)

Wealth and Welfare or Our National Trade Policy and Its Cost (1887)

British Industries and Foreign Competition (1894)

Perils to British Trade: How to Avert Them (1895)

From the standpoint of the historian, two works are particularly valuable for the light they throw on the economic difficulties of the late Victorian generation: Ernest E. Williams' *"Made in Germany"* (1896) and Fred A. McKenzie's *The American Invaders: Their Plans, Tactics and Progress* (1902). Both volumes gave rise to much discussion and criticism and helped to clarify and shape popular thinking about England's economic future.

The German Threat. *"Made in Germany,"* one of the most widely read late Victorian books on economics, has often been cited as evidence of the gloom that descended on Englishmen as a result of the progress of German industry and commerce. This, however, is a half-truth that ignores the optimism with which Williams approached the problem of German economic competition. He was convinced that if the English knew why Germany was beating them and proceeded to apply the appropriate remedies, they could be saved. His was a message of hope, not of despair; a warning, as he put it, was "more useful than an obituary notice." The people he wanted chiefly to alert were the manufacturers and merchants of the United Kingdom, to whom he dedicated his book. Williams left no doubt that England's economic supremacy, so long a commonplace, was departing; it was rapidly becoming a myth "as inappropriate to fact as the Chinese Emperor's computation of his own status." Unfortunately, the English people were insufficiently aware of either the damage already done or the dangers impending. To disturb this "fatal torpor" was one of Williams' main objectives—

the more so because orthodox political economists, imbued with free trade doctrines, were failing to undertake the task. Instead of rousing the late Victorians, they were flattering and deluding them. By their refusal to acknowledge what was rotten in the English economy, they demonstrated the poverty of their patriotism.

In practically all English industries Williams detected a steady slowing down. No longer "the Universal Provider," the English were finding their iron, steel, ships, hardware, machines, cutlery, textiles, chemicals, toys, leather goods, musical instruments, paper, glass, earthenware, printing, and other products in heavy competition with the goods of Germans, who were bent on the extinction of English supremacy. The trouble was, however, that too many people viewed Germany as an industrial infant and England as an industrial giant, and "to tell a strong man, conscious of his strength to an over-weening degree, that he is in peril from a half-grown youngster, is to invite his derision." Williams' point was that "if a strong man, as the years advance on him, neglect himself and abuse his strength, he may fall before an energetic stripling." The English, in short, must realize that "on all hands England's industrial supremacy is tottering to its fall, and that this result is largely German work." (*See Document No. 8.*)

Why Germany Was Advancing.   What mattered to Williams was not so much that England was deteriorating economically but rather that the tendency could be stopped. Certainly the English must not think that Germany was winning because of the low wages of her workers and their long hours of labor. Williams doubted that German wages were lower and hours of work longer than those of the English. Even if they were, he believed that lower productivity would be the result. Similarly, Williams was unwilling to consider strikes a significant factor in the waning of English industrial supremacy, but he recognized the danger that, while English strikes were taking place, the Germans could move into what were traditionally English markets.

According to Williams, what really counted was the help which German businessmen received from the state. Tariffs made it possible for German manufacturers to

flood England with their goods. Since their products
were protected in Germany, they were able, when necessary, to sell them elsewhere even below the cost of production. Along with tariffs went bounties, subsidies, relatively cheap transportation, a consular system whose
members did not consider it undignified to serve as agents
of German firms, and a most remarkable tradition of
technical education. Ironically, however, the stereotype of
the Germans was that they were a people "devoted to
dreamy philosophy or plodding research into remote by-
paths of knowledge; a people addicted to the piling up of
facts of little use to any one, and least of all to their
compilers."

How to Beat Germany. It was not only state help
that explained the growing economic leadership of Germany; self-help also had much to do with it. German
businessmen had "push," the word which, to Williams,
suggested the cause of "perhaps the biggest part of
Germany's success." Along with the businessman's push
went his adaptability. He was tactful and determined to
please his customers. If, therefore, the economic decline
of England was to be averted, it was necessary for the
English people to understand that there was much they
could learn from the Germans. Williams granted that
some of the harm already done was irreparable; there
was, after all, no likelihood that Germany would cease to
be an industrial state. Yet if the English undertook certain specific steps, much that was rotten in commercial
and industrial England could be removed. The English
must reconsider their tariff policy, for protection was responsible for many of Germany's economic strides.
Williams was well aware that in "the present state of general opinion" the abandonment of England's free trade
policy would represent a revolutionary change and that
therefore "one almost shrinks from reference to it." Conscious that he was endangering the popularity of his general appeal, he, nevertheless, endorsed the principle of
reciprocity: however much English goods were penalized
in a foreign country, so much should the goods of that
country be penalized in England. Similarly, he defended
the idea of imperial federation in economic matters:
England and the colonies should admit one another's

products on terms more favorable than those of foreign
countries.

Williams had great faith in the results that he thought
would flow from an overhauling of the consular system.
If the number of commercial attachés was greatly increased and if they were taught that their main responsibility was to help English traders by gathering information about changing fashions and needs, they could
contribute substantially to the prosperity of the English
economy. Williams was especially enthusiastic about a
reform of the consular service because it would cost little
and would not stir up the various vested interests.

Another much needed reform, technical education,
would both arouse pressure groups and cost a good deal,
but it was of such importance that all objections to it had
to be set aside. True, the English had by and large gotten
along without technical schools. In view of German
rivalry, however, they needed the best practical and
theoretical training possible. To complain of the expense
was suicidal. Lady Bracknell had rejoiced in *The Importance of Being Earnest* (1895) that education in
England produced "no effect whatsoever." Williams
wanted it to have enormous effects. He found it imperative to attack the practice of making elementary education mainly literary: "Learning the names of Canaanitish
chiefs and the like gymnastics of the mind might with
advantage make room for elementary instruction in some
useful or beautiful craft."

Tariff reform, changes in the consular system, and the
expansion of technical education were indispensable. Yet
Williams was the first to insist that state help was not
enough to stem the inroads that the Germans were making. Self-help was also vital. English merchants and manufacturers must learn the meaning of enterprise in this new
age of economic rivalries. They must pay more attention
to the tastes and needs of their customers. They must
adopt the metric system for their export business. They
must employ traveling salesmen familiar with the languages of the areas they covered. They must stop sneer-
ing at small orders. They must learn the importance of
careful packing and of similar details involved in an
efficiently run business. They must keep their equipment

up to date. They must emphasize graceful form and pleasing design in their products. They must advertise more effectively. They must avoid labor troubles, remembering that well-paid workers are the best. All in all, English businessmen must be progressive in their outlook and ready to employ new discoveries and to adjust constantly to the changes in the needs of their customers. Williams was convinced that if the English combined state help and self-help, they could achieve excellent results. There was no possibility of restoring their position as unchallenged leaders of the world economy, but at least their relative position in economic affairs could be improved.

"Made in Germany" appeared at a propitious time. Its success was due in no small measure to the fears generated by the long, drawn-out depression as well as to the deterioration of Anglo-German diplomatic relations that occurred in the mid-nineties. This is not to deny that the book itself had considerable merit. While it lacked originality, it drew heavily on the voluminous reports of parliamentary investigating committees, and it presented their findings with accuracy, coherence, unity, emphasis, and forceful prose. So strictly did Williams adhere to his theme that none of his contemporaries could have gathered from his book that he was a member of that despised minority—the Socialists.

Made in the United States. All was not lost—this was the essence of Williams' message to his countrymen in 1896. A few years later in a strikingly similar book, *The American Invaders: Their Plans, Tactics and Progress,* Fred A. McKenzie preached the same gospel of hope. If English manufacturers and merchants were made aware of the need for immediate action and if they bestirred themselves, McKenzie was convinced that there still could be a happy future for the English economy. Things at the moment did not look bright, to be sure. As McKenzie put it: "To-day it is literally true that Americans are selling their cottons in Manchester, pig-iron in Lancashire, and steel in Sheffield. They send oatmeal to Scotland, potatoes to Ireland, and our national beef to England. It only remains for them to take coals to Newcastle. In fact, the time seems coming when, as an American wittily put it, we shall find our chief export across the Atlantic to be scions of our own nobility, whom America cannot produce on account of the limits imposed by her constitution. And, even there, the balance of trade will be in America's favor, for she sends us her gracious daughters to grace our ducal homes."

In industry after industry the English were losing out to the Americans, and in their search for markets English merchants were being defeated by American energy, initiative, and brains. It was bad enough that the signs of English economic decay were unmistakable in such old enterprises as the iron, shipping, cotton, and coal industries. Worse still, McKenzie correctly noted, Americans were showing singular skill in virtually all the new industries that were emerging, and many of these were highly profitable. Americans were making telephones, cameras, phonographs, electric street cars, automobiles, typewriters, elevators, machine tools, and hundreds of other relatively new products. Like Williams, McKenzie emphasized that English manufacturers and merchants must understand the reasons for the growing economic success of foreign powers. Americans, he insisted, drove themselves much more than their happy-go-lucky English competitors. They worked harder and longer. They were more willing to take risks. Their superior education, he said, prepared them to receive new ideas more readily. They did not hold on to antiquated equipment; on the contrary, they spent much money to improve their machines and keep them up to date. Not only were they less hampered by tradition than the English, but they constantly looked to the future, trying to anticipate demands for new products. And they did not hesitate to call for government aid in the form of protective tariffs.

The English could learn much from recent American economic progress. They could break the habit of resting on their reputation. They could stop being so easygoing, so conservative, so unwilling to experiment. They could get rid of the "Good-Enough-for-Grandfather" spirit. They could learn to use the weapons of their competitors. English merchants and manufacturers, in a word, had only to rouse themselves in earnest. They would then be in a position to recover some of the ground they had lost, and the American invasion of English markets would turn out to be a blessing.

A Bleak Future. Unlike McKenzie and Williams, many late Victorian businessmen feared the future. (*See Document No. 9.*) They considered it inevitable that they would continue to fall behind ambitious and methodical Germans and alert and aggressive Americans, and they found plenty of statistics to justify and to bolster their gloom. They knew that their methods were obsolete and their machinery antiquated, but they were often in no position to make changes. Some simply went bankrupt. Some joined combinations, popularly called trusts, which sought to limit and control competition, raise prices, and increase profits. Some pinned their hopes on the protectionist agitation that went by the name of fair trade. As one historian of this movement has pointed out, the founders of the Fair Trade League included "a sugar refiner, a banker and publisher with interests in iron and steel, a manufacturer of silks, and another manufacturer of woolens and worsteds." Other businessmen viewed the return to protection as economically undesirable or as politically impossible. But whether the members of the business community agreed or disagreed about tariffs as a remedy for hard times, they agreed by and large about the hard times. They would have applauded those members of the Royal Commission who complained that its Final Report was unduly optimistic and that it did not stress sufficiently the unprofitable conditions under which commerce and industry were carried on. They would have been outraged by the knowledge that some economists of their own day and many in later years would belittle and even deny the existence of the depression from which they suffered.

4

THE CONDITION OF
THE WORKING CLASSES

Partisan Views. The condition of urban workers in the age of the great depression, like that of rural laborers, has been much debated. Already in 1886 the Royal Commission on the Depression of Trade and Industry pointed out that the evidence it had accumulated concerning the position of the working classes was filled with contradictory opinions. Since then views on the subject have continued to conflict. Writers sympathetic to capitalism have tended to emphasize the gains the late Victorian worker achieved and to underrate the hardships from which he suffered. Writers hostile to capitalism have tended to stress his hardships and to minimize his gains. The subject, in short, is a difficult one, but the historian should try to estimate the validity of the claims of both groups of partisans.

The Brighter Side. In several important respects the worker improved his economic position during the late Victorian period. To start with, he could buy more commodities in the late 1890's than in the early 1870's, for not only had his nominal or money wages risen but the prices he paid for goods had fallen. Statistical estimates of real wages differ for the period; some are more glowing than others. But there can be no doubt that as the late Victorian years passed the typical worker earned more and his earnings purchased more. He consumed greater quantities of tea, sugar, meat, beer, and tobacco than ever before, he could buy more clothes more often, and he could afford to pay for somewhat better housing facilities.

He also spent less time at his job. True, the number of hours he labored was rarely an accurate test of the arduousness of his work, but in a period when moralists stressed the importance of leisure not only for rest, relaxa-

tion, and better family relations but for self-improvement
and what was called "the higher life," it was inevitable
that agitation would develop to shorten the work week.
Back in 1870 the average worker devoted about sixty
hours to his job. By the end of Victoria's reign the
figure was down in many instances to about fifty-four.
According to the Final Report of the Royal Commission
on Labour, issued in 1894, skilled workers and unskilled
laborers who worked with them rarely put in more than a
nine-hour day, and the Commission recognized how widespread the movement for an eight-hour day was becoming.

Not only was the worker devoting fewer hours to his
job, but the likelihood was that he labored under better
conditions. Already in 1880 he was favored by a law that
provided for accident insurance, and this measure was
extended and strengthened towards the end of the century. Furthermore, he no longer had to compete so much
as in the past with cheap labor, for the age at which a
child could start to work in a factory or workshop was
steadily raised in the late Victorian period. In other ways,
too, the worker found his condition improved. Because of
the enactment of a series of educational reforms starting
in 1870, he could provide his children with elementary
education, and literacy encouraged hopes for a brighter
future. The worker also benefited by the increase in the
number of parks, libraries, public baths, and public
hospitals as well as from improved sanitation and better
police and fire protection.

Fortunately for the historian, several of the best-
informed late Victorian economists set forth their views
on the position of the working classes. In his inaugural
address as president of the Statistical Society, Robert
Giffen emphasized in 1883 that "while the individual incomes of the working classes have largely increased, the
prices of the main articles of their consumption have
rather declined; and the inference as to their being much
better off which would be drawn from these facts is fully
supported by statistics showing a decline in the rate of
mortality, an increase of the consumption of articles in
general use, an improvement in general education, a
diminution of crime and pauperism, a vast increase of the

number of depositors in savings banks, and other evidences of general well-being." A few years later, in another address on the progress of the working classes, Giffen said: "From being a dependent class without future and hope, the masses of working men have in fact got into a position from which they may effectually advance to almost any degree of civilisation. Every agency, political and other, should be made use of by themselves and others to promote and extend the improvement. But the working men have the game in their own hands. Education and thrift, which they can achieve for themselves, will, if necessary, do all that remains to be done." This, too, was the view of Leone Levi, Professor of the Principles and Practice of Commerce in King's College, London. In a work on *Wages and Earnings of the Working Classes* (1885), prepared for the guidance of a member of Parliament, Levi emphasized the great strides that workers were making. They were much better off than their English predecessors and their foreign contemporaries. (*See Document No. 10.*)

Workers' Hardships.   All this is not to belittle the hardships of the laboring classes in the last decades of the nineteenth century. Indeed, those late Victorian writers who dealt with the working-class world in their novels and short stories—Sir Walter Besant, George Gissing, Arthur Morrison, Israel Zangwill, and the young Somerset Maugham—usually stressed its seamier side. At times they wrote under the influence of Emile Zola's naturalism. More often, they simply continued in the tradition of such earlier proletarian novels as Disraeli's *Sybil,* Mrs. Gaskell's *Mary Barton,* Charles Kingsley's *Yeast* and *Alton Locke,* Dickens' *Hard Times,* Charles Reade's *It Is Never Too Late to Mend,* and George Eliot's *Felix Holt, the Radical.* Generally, they wrote as reformers. They considered it a function of imaginative literature to expose abuses, and they certainly found many to expose.

In the absence of state-sponsored schemes of insurance, workers lived in dread of sickness and old age. Above all, they feared unemployment—and with good cause. For in several peak years—1879, 1886, 1894—it reached alarming proportions. On an overall basis, however, the unemployment rate was less than five per cent in the late Victorian period. It was, in other words, about the same as in early and post-Victorian times. Even so, the fear of unemployment and underemployment was universal among late Victorian workers. Nor was this surprising, for, however willing they were to work, they remained at the mercy of fluctuations in the business cycle, seasonal variations, the disorganization of the labor market, the ruin of individual industries, the introduction of labor-saving techniques, the movement of firms from one area to another, and other causes of unemployment. In the words of a silk weaver who, on complaining, had been reminded that all people have their problems: ". . . troubles are a deal easier to bear when you've good food and fires and clothes, and no likelihood of losing of 'em. Whatever sorrows you've had, you've never had the sorrow of a hungry belly, and half-a-dozen more hungry bellies round you that belong to ye!" William Morris knew what he was doing when in one of his Socialist poems he appealed to workers with these lines:

> Men in that time a'coming shall work and have no fear.
> For to-morrow's lack of earning and the hunger-wolf anear.
>
> I tell you this for a wonder, that no man then shall be glad
> Of his fellow's fall and mishap to snatch at the work he had.

Sweated Workers. There were other hardships that affected sections of the late Victorian laboring classes. By the standards of the age, sweated workers—those engaged, usually at home, in the manufacture of slop clothing, inferior shoes and slippers, cheap chairs and cabinets, and crude nails, files, and cutlery—led a particularly degraded existence. Lacking the protection of factory acts and trade unions, they worked unbelievably long hours for very low pay and under shockingly unwholesome circumstances. When the Select Committee of the House of Lords on the Sweating System drew up its report, it expressed the hope that the evils it exposed would "induce capitalists to pay closer attention to the conditions under which the labour which supplies them with goods is conducted." These conditions, however, were not as a rule the fault of individual capitalists. If, as Tennyson put it, "the master scrimp[ed] his haggard sempstress of her daily bread," the reason was that the sweated industries were highly competitive. In order to survive the entrepreneur had to keep his cost of production very low. From the standpoint of labor the difficulty was that the sweated industries required little or no skill; the work was so subdivided that it could easily be learned. Almost anybody could work in a sweated industry, and many did. (*See Document No. 11.*) Ida Starr, the heroine of George Gissing's novel, *The Unclassed* (1884), preferred prostitution to a health-destroying sweated trade.

The White Slaves of England. Along with the sweated workers, the most pathetic figures in the late Victorian working-class world were those engaged in particularly dangerous industries: alkali and white-lead workers, for example. Indeed, these people, along with nailmakers, chainmakers, slipper-makers, and wool-combers, figured as *The White Slaves of England* (1897) in a sensational book by Robert Sherard. The volume was frequently quoted all over the world in order to publicize the dangers and horrors of English working-class life. Not surprisingly, it infuriated young Rudyard Kipling to hear Liberals talk about British oppression of the natives in India—when at home "white girls of sixteen, at twelve or fourteen pounds per annum, hauled thirty and forty pounds weight of bath-water at a time up four flights of stairs!" And it incensed George Bernard Shaw that so many of his contemporaries attributed prostitution to depravity and licentiousness. He believed that it was caused by poverty, and he wrote one of his early plays, *Mrs. Warren's Profession* (1894), to prove his thesis. He had Mrs. Warren explain that, rather than work in a white-lead factory twelve hours a day for nine shillings a week and die of lead poisoning as one of her sisters did, she became a prostitute.

Finally, among the lowliest elements of English society, there was that vague mass of down-and-outers about whom General William Booth wrote in his widely-read *In*

Darkest England, and the Way Out (1890) and to whom
Charles Booth, starting in 1889, called attention in his
epoch-making studies of the life and labor of Londoners.
These were the human animals whom the Royal Commission on Labour classified as "still a deplorably large
residuum of the population, chiefly to be found in our
large cities, who lead wretchedly poor lives, and are
seldom far removed from the level of starvation." The
Commission added that, fortunately, they were declining
in number both relatively and absolutely, but it was such
people, among others, whom the Socialist journalist,
Robert Blatchford, had in mind when he asked his readers
to suppose that a child "is born in a poor hovel, in a
poor slum. Suppose its home surroundings are such that
cleanliness and modesty are well-nigh impossible. Suppose the gutter is its playground; the ginshop its nursery;
the factory its college; the drunkard its exemplar; the
ruffian and the thief its instructors! Suppose bad nursing,
bad air, bad water, bad food, dirt, hunger, ill-usage, foul
language, and hard work are its daily portion. Suppose it
has inherited poor blood, dull spirits, enfeebled wit, and
a stunted stature, from its ill-fed, untaught, overworked,
miserable, ignorant, and unhealthy parents, can you expect that child to be clever, and moral, and thrifty, and
clean, and sober?"

Despite the sufferings of the poorest sections of the
laboring classes, the general record of workers' accomplishments in the late Victorian age was impressive to
contemporaries. Giffen was correct when he kept using
the word progress in his discussions of labor conditions;
and that indefatigable enemy of socialism, W. H. Mallock,
exaggerated only slightly when in his *Classes and Masses,
or Wealth, Wages, and Welfare in the United Kingdom*
(1896) he called the recent progress of the worker "probably the most extraordinary phenomenon in the social history of the world." For, all things considered, the average
worker was much better off in the late 1890's than he had
been in the early 1870's. But though his position improved rapidly, it did not keep pace with humanitarian
conceptions of what that position should be. As Tennyson
asked in 1886:

> Is it well that while we range with Science, glorying
>   in the Time,
> City children soak and blacken soul and sense in city
>   slime?

And as a witness before the Royal Commission on Labour put it: "I think the condition of the working classes has changed immensely, but not so much, I am happy to say, as the change in public opinion on the subjects relating to that class." Sir Walter Besant was right when among the greatest gains of the Victorian age he singled out what he called "the growth of sympathy with all those who suffer, whether wrongfully or by misfortune, or through their own misdoings."

Trade Unions Grow.   The improvements that took place in the status of late Victorian workers were due, among many other causes, to rising productivity, the growth of consumers' and producers' coöperatives, the humanitarian activities of the middle and upper classes, and state intervention. Workers themselves were often inclined to attribute their rising standard of living above all to the growth of trade unionism. In 1872 there were fewer than 400,000 union members, and they were as a rule highly skilled. By the end of Victoria's reign there were almost 2,000,000 members, a goodly proportion of whom were classed as unskilled. In the intervening years, trade union membership varied—sometimes sharply—in keeping with fluctuations in the business cycle, but at no time in the late Victorian age did it represent more than a small portion of the total laboring force. Women workers in particular remained outside the union movement. A Women's Trades Union League was formed in 1874 by Emma Paterson, a pioneer in the slowly growing women's rights movement. But her efforts were largely unsuccessful. Women lacked interest in combining for many reasons but above all, perhaps, because they expected to marry, and they considered marriage, often wrongly as it turned out, a release from competition in the labor market. What John Stuart Mill and others were fond of calling "the subjection of women" was in part made possible by the weakness of women's trade unions. Students of the working classes have placed too much emphasis on the differences in late Victorian times be-

tween the old unions of skilled workers and the new
unions of relatively unskilled workers. The fact is that
both kinds of organizations served as benefit and friendly
societies, making funds available to workers in the event
of sickness, accident, and unemployment. And both old
and new unions had the same economic objectives: to
keep wages high, to prevent hours of work from being
what was regarded as excessive, to limit unemployment
by distributing available work as much as possible among
members, to improve generally the conditions of labor,
and to afford protection against the type of employer who
regarded his workers as mere machines to be exploited to
the utmost regardless of the effects of such treatment on
them. Despite the presence of a few Socialists among
the leaders of the new unions, the mass of the membership of both old and new unions accepted the capitalist
system; they simply wanted a larger slice of the profits.

Hostility to Unionism. Some unions were, to be
sure, more successful than others in achieving their main
economic aims, but successful or not they were widely
criticized and feared in business circles. The eminent
economist, W. Stanley Jevons, had cautioned that just
as "we should certainly not condemn the whole aristocracy because a few of its members are convicted of
crime, or misconduct, or folly, so we should still less
assail the character of such a vast number of men as the
united operatives of England, because some of their
number have been concerned in deeds which we cannot
approve." Many employers felt differently. They were
convinced that union leaders were not only agitators but
embezzlers, blackmailers, and charlatans, and they feared
such would-be masters. They thought unions existed only
in order to cause strikes, and they believed that union
funds were devoted above all to the prolongation of
strikes. They attributed their low profits in the age of
the great depression to the growth of trade union strength,
they insisted that unions were making workers lazy and
irresponsible, and they envied foreign businessmen who
could bargain individually with their labor. Their attitude
was in no small measure responsible for the formation
of the Labour Party. (*See Document No. 12.*)

Marx Refuted. Karl Marx had expected great

things from English workers. They lived and worked, after all, in the chief center of the industrial capitalist world—in what he called the "demiurge of the bourgeois cosmos." Marx was convinced that the conflict between capitalists and workers had to be settled in England, and he based *Das Kapital* in large measure on his reading of the English historical experience. So powerful was English capitalism that if it were overthrown, this example would hasten the repudiation of capitalism in other countries. Marx considered the triumph of English workers over their employers "decisive for the victory of all oppressed people over their oppressors," and he counted on an economic depression to render the revolution certain. It came, but it brought about no revolution. Late Victorian economic history, in fact, falsified Marx's basic predictions. His law of capital accumulations—that the means of production were to be owned by fewer and fewer people—and his law of increasing misery—that the poor were to become poorer—failed to operate. In the words of a thoughtful student of the subject: "Plainly the social movement of England presented very difficult problems to Marx. He grew more pessimistic with the passing years." That events in England did not work out according to the Marxist dream was due in part to the great depression with its falling prices and rising real wages.

5

THE STATE AN ENEMY

The Depression and Politics. Farmers, landowners, merchants, manufacturers, and urban and rural workers —all could have testified to the effects of the depression of 1873-1896 on their lives. Yet the depression shaped not only the social and economic history of the late Victorians; it also had impressive repercussions on their political and intellectual development. It influenced significantly the growth of state intervention and the debates to which it gave rise, the Irish Question and the controversies it precipitated, and the renewed emphasis on imperialism and the conflicts it provoked.

Long before the coming of the depression in the early 1870's, the state had been expanding its powers. Indeed, the period from about 1830 to about 1870, which has often been singled out as the heyday of the do-little state, was not that at all. Government after government passed law after law that defied and modified the creed of individualism and self-help. This interventionist tradition, already well established in pre-Victorian and early Victorian times, was continued and strengthened in the age of the great depression. It is significant that when the Royal Commission on Agriculture was appointed in 1879 it was specifically authorized "to inquire into the depressed condition of the Agricultural interest, and the causes to which it is owing; whether those causes are of a permanent character, and how far they have been created or can be remedied by legislation." Similarly, the Royal Commission on Agriculture, appointed in 1893, was given the responsibility of determining whether the agricultural depression could be "alleviated by legislation or other measures." Such instances can readily be multiplied.

This is not to say that all or nearly all measures of government intervention in the late Victorian age were the products of the depression. The growing disposition to legislate on almost every phase of social life was perhaps above all related to the extension of the franchise. The point is, though, that the depression encouraged more and more people—some of whom in the past had been arch-individualists—to favor state help. Not surprisingly, believers in *laissez-faire* complained that "we now hear it constantly stated at public meetings that the continued depression of trade renders it absolutely necessary for the Government to 'do something.' "

For centuries legislation had been only one of several functions that Parliament performed. By the time the nineteenth century ended there could be no doubt that it was by far its most important function. Interventionist legislation took a bewildering variety of forms in the late Victorian age, and there is no better way to become aware of this variety than by paging through the successive volumes of the *Public General Acts.*

Parliament in Action. The late Victorians became so accustomed to having laws passed on almost every conceivable subject that Captain Fitzbattleaxe in Gilbert and Sullivan's *Utopia, Limited* (1893) could even invent the Rival Admirers' Clauses Consolidation Act, which, he explained, dealt with standard procedure when two gentlemen loved the same lady.

In the 1870's, when Gladstone and Disraeli served as Prime Ministers, measures were enacted to extend the laws concerning factories and workshops, to provide for public elementary education, to facilitate the construction and to regulate the working of tramways, to reform the laws relating to the property of married women, to regularize the liquidation of joint stock and other companies, to encourage gifts of land for public parks, schools, and museums, to improve the status of trade unions, to make more effective the inspection and regulation of railways, to provide for arbitration between masters and workmen, to prevent the adulteration of food, drink, and drugs, to regulate coal and other mines, to supervise the employment of children in agriculture, to stimulate the construction and improvement of dwellings for the working classes, to reform the laws concerning sanitation and public health, to facilitate the transfer of land, to stop the use of unseaworthy ships, to better the

position of friendly societies, to afford facilities for the
enjoyment by the public of open spaces in London, to
further the growth of public libraries, public baths, and
washhouses, to prevent the introduction and spread of
crop-destroying insects, to avoid accidents by threshing
machines, to halt the adulteration of seeds, to consolidate
the law relating to weights and measures, to combat the
contagious and infectious diseases of cattle and other
animals, and to control and cure habitual drunkards.

In the 1880's, when Gladstone and Salisbury headed
ministries, interventionist legislation dealt once more with
a vast array of subjects. Laws were passed to extend the
liability of employers to make compensation for personal
injuries suffered by workmen in their service, to protect
occupiers of land against injury to their crops from
ground game, to supervise alkali and other works where
poisonous gases were present, to make better provision
for inquiries into boiler explosions, to promote the improvement of settled land, to regulate the supply of
electricity for lighting, to consolidate the law concerning
the property of married women, to prohibit the payment
of wages to workmen in public houses, to isolate and
treat people suffering from cholera and other infectious
diseases, to suppress brothels, to provide facilities for the
care, education, and training of idiots and imbeciles, to
limit the hours of work of children and young persons in
shops, to compensate the occupiers of allotments and
cottage gardens for crops left in the ground at the end of
their tenancies, to stimulate the provision of allotments
for the laboring classes, to control the sale of horsemeat
for human food, to establish a Board of Agriculture, to
prevent cruelty to children, to improve the regulation of
cotton cloth factories, and to further the provision of
technical instruction.

In the 1890's, when Salisbury, Gladstone, and Rosebery
served as prime ministers, legislative intervention was
again far-reaching. Kelvil, the M.P. in Oscar Wilde's
A Woman of No Importance (1893), was right to point
out that "the demands on the time of a public man are
very heavy now-a-days, very heavy indeed." There were
acts to encourage gifts of land for working-class dwellings, to enable urban authorities to establish and maintain

museums and gymnasiums, to advance public elementary education, to extend the laws concerning factories and workshops, to stimulate the acquisition of small agricultural holdings, to make better provision for the elementary education of blind, deaf, and epileptic children, to achieve the more effective regulation of quarries, to consolidate legislation concerning merchant shipping, to encourage the peaceful settlement of trade disputes, to improve the laws dealing with workmen's compensation, to increase the age below which the employment of young people in dangerous occupations was prohibited, to forbid the importation from foreign countries of prison-made goods, to provide seats for shop assistants, to establish a Board of Education, and to enable people to become owners of the small houses in which they lived.

Local Government Thrives. Late Victorian parliaments also enacted fiscal legislation which relieved the poor increasingly of the burden of taxation. Furthermore, quite apart from a mass of public general acts, late Victorian parliaments passed hundreds of local measures dealing with social and economic subjects. Local governmental authorities, thus legally armed, proceeded to intervene with gusto in the lives of their citizens. In the words of Princess Zara of *Utopia, Limited:*

> This County Councillor acclaim,
>   Great Britain's latest toy—
> On anything you like to name
>   His talents he'll employ—
>
> All streets and squares he'll purify
>   Within your city walls,
> And keep meanwhile a modest eye
>   On wicked music halls.

The County Councillor answered:

> Yes—yes—yes—
> In towns I make improvements great,
> Which go to swell the County Rate—
> I dwelling-houses sanitate,
>   And purify the Halls!

Even so humorless a critic of self-help as Sidney Webb could write: "The Individualist Town Councillor will walk along the municipal pavement, lit by municipal gas and cleansed by municipal brooms with municipal water, and seeing by the municipal clock in the municipal market, that he is too early to meet his children coming from the municipal school hard by the county lunatic asylum and municipal hospital, will use the national telegraph system to tell them not to walk through the municipal park but to come by the municipal tramway, to meet him in the municipal reading room, by the municipal art gallery, museum and library, where he intends to consult some of the national publications in order to prepare his next speech in the municipal town-hall, in favour of the nationalization of canals and the increase of the government control over the railway system. 'Socialism, sir,' he will say, 'don't waste the time of a practical man by your fantastic absurdities. Self-help, sir, individual self-help, that's what's made our city what it is.' "

Whether the Conservatives or the Liberals were in power did not matter; both parties contributed to the growth of state intervention. As one Victorian newspaperman, referring to some Conservative measures of social reform, said: "Great objects no doubt; but objects which stand equally in the policy of the Liberal party." True, the Conservatives held sway in the late Victorian period for more years than the Liberals, and so present-day Conservatives have been able to remind voters of the long-standing Tory tradition of social welfare legislation. The fact is, though, that late Victorian Liberals also enacted important measures of social and economic reform, and they coöperated in passing legislation under Conservative leadership. The behavior of both parties reflected the influence of the great depression and a democratic suffrage. Queen Victoria protested that she could not and would not be a democratic monarch, but her protest was futile, especially in an age of depression.

The Battle Against Legislative Meddling. Middle and upper-class Victorians who believed in a do-little state were alarmed by the extension of the sphere of government that took place in the last decades of the nineteenth century, for they equated state intervention with socialism. Some of them organized the Liberty and Property

Defence League, hoping that it would have as successful a
record in combating legislative meddling as the famous
Anti-Corn Law League had had in fighting protective
tariffs. Although the Liberty and Property Defence
League was often denounced by its opponents as a society
of Tory reactionaries, it was not concerned with party
politics as such. It welcomed Tories, Liberals, and members of any party who viewed the state as the enemy and
believed that government best which governed least. (*See
Documents No. 13 and No. 14.*)

Property Is Sacred. Finding self-interest the main-
spring of human behavior, members of the League were
certain that the more people were permitted to rely on
their own exertions, the more the wealth of the community would grow. Members of the League were equally
certain that whatever progress had occurred in the course
of human history was the result of liberty and property.
To assure progress in the future was, therefore, relatively
easy: the sacredness and interdependence of liberty and
property had to be recognized; state interference had to
be kept down to a minimum; and self-help, rather than
state help, had to be encouraged. Their reading of history
assured Leaguers of the folly of attempting by legislative
enactments to resist the operation of economic laws, and
they bemoaned the fact that what to them was an
eternal truth was not universally grasped. Nothing would
have made them happier than the dissolution of their
organization, but that could happen only when property
owners ceased to be the playthings of politicians and
slaves of the state and when the propertyless elements in
society learned the virtues of individualism. Such a time,
unfortunately, seemed far off. In the words of one leader
of the League: "You have another king, another tyrant,
to deal with now. His name is Demos, and he is ignorant,
as a rule. He is fickle, predatory in his tendencies, and
gullible in the extreme, believing always the biggest liar
or the man who will promise him most of his neighbours'
goods as the right reward of his support or vote." Like
George Gissing, W. E. H. Lecky, and other late Victorian critics of democracy, Leaguers condemned senti-
mental exaltation of the masses.

The League carried on its educational campaign with

energy and zeal worthy of a society of missionaries. Working on the assumption that growing state power was a world problem, it encouraged the formation of federated societies not only in England, Scotland, Ireland, and the Empire but in the United States, France, Italy, Germany, and Switzerland. It brought out pamphlets, leaflets, and books explaining its principles, and among the publications issued under its auspices were works with such titles as *The Fallacies and Follies of Socialist-Radicalism Exposed, Radicalism and Its Stupidities, Equality: A Socialist-Radical Fallacy, Justice for England: Or, How to Fight Socialism, The Socialist Spectre*, and *The Pretensions of Socialism*. The League even went so far as to invite interested non-members to submit for consideration any publishable manuscripts that stressed the dangers of legislative meddling. Similarly, it gave publicity to journals like *The Liberty Review, The Whirlwind, The Free Life, The Personal Rights Journal*, and *The Trumpet*, all of which stressed the glories of individualism. The League also conducted a department which provided speakers for public meetings. These lecturers explained the principles of the League and mobilized opposition to any objectionable legislation that was pending. Perhaps most important, the League organized a Parliamentary Committee which, whenever Parliament was in session, issued special lists of the bills it considered undesirable. It distributed copies of these lists among members of Parliament, the press, the federated societies, and the public. As each objectionable bill came up for consideration, the committee took whatever steps it found necessary to defeat the measure.

The Victorian Aristotle. It was no surprise that members of the League regarded Herbert Spencer as the outstanding intellectual in late Victorian England. If they took pride in labelling him "our modern Aristotle," it was not only for his contributions to sociology, psychology, education, and other fields; it was, above all, because of his hostility to government intervention. Already in the 1840's, Spencer had expressed his views on the proper sphere of government, and he continued to do so during the course of a long life. His most forceful statement of his case against the theory and practice of state help appeared in a series of four articles originally published in

1884 in the *Contemporary Review* and reprinted in the same year as a book with the title *The Man Versus the State*. Spencer was alarmed by the drift of Victorian legislation, and he hoped to awaken his countrymen to its dangers. "Regulations," he warned, "have been made in yearly-growing numbers, restraining the citizen in directions where his actions were previously unchecked, and compelling actions which previously he might perform or not as he liked; and at the same time heavier public burdens, chiefly local, have further restricted his freedom, by lessening that portion of his earnings which he can spend as he pleases, and augmenting the portion taken from him to be spent as public agents please."

What disturbed Spencer was the fact that both leading political parties were becoming more and more interventionist. The Tories, to be sure, had long advocated government interference in the life of the individual; according to Spencer, what distinguished them historically was their defense of the coercive power of the state over the subject. Liberals, on the other hand, had a tradition of respect for the idea and practice of self-help; what distinguished them historically was their constant effort to diminish the range of government regulation and to increase the area within which each individual could act without interference. The only restraints Liberals placed on the individual were those "needful for preventing him from directly or indirectly aggressing on his fellows—needful, that is, for maintaining the liberties of his fellows against his invasions of them."

Spencer's view of the past rôle of Conservatives and Liberals was a gross oversimplification of a complicated history, and his conception of valid restraints was dangerously elastic. Such objections to the case he was making do not matter too much, however. He was drawing lessons from the past only in order to throw light on the present. The point he was trying to make was that the Liberals were abandoning their traditions—so much so, that more and more they were becoming "new Tories." Like their historical opponents, they were dictating the actions of the citizen and curtailing his freedom. Instead of promoting human welfare through the relaxation of restraints, they stood increasingly for state coercion. With

Liberals and Conservatives vying with each other in limiting the freedom of the citizen, the believer in self-help found himself deserted. However reluctantly, he was forced to recognize that both political parties were filled with politicians who believed that the government should step in whenever things were going wrong. Nor was this surprising, for now that the masses could vote, parliamentary candidates attempted to assure their election by proposing and supporting all kinds of new laws, and they outdid each other in making outrageous promises to voters.

The Poor Cause Their Own Poverty. Spencer resented the sympathetic attitude towards the poor that was becoming so widespread in late Victorian society. As far as he was concerned, the poor deserved, for the most part, to be poor. The authors of their own misery, they were paying the price of their misconduct—their refusal to work or to hold on to a job. Spencer regarded them simply as good-for-nothings whose main ambition was to live at the expense of the good-for-somethings. To Spencer it was absurd for people to think that all hardships either could or should be prevented. He viewed suffering as a cure that would encourage the poor to help themselves. It was obvious to him that the more the government intervened, the more people would expect and demand that it intervene. He insisted that "the more numerous public instrumentalities become, the more is there generated in citizens the notion that everything is to be done for them, and nothing by them. Each generation is made less familiar with the attainment of desired ends by individual actions or private combinations, and more familiar with the attainment of them by governmental agencies; until, eventually, governmental agencies come to be thought of as the only available agencies."

Spencer was far more sophisticated than many of his twentieth-century critics would have people believe. He knew that he was defending a cause that had long been lost and that for his efforts he would be "reviled as a reactionary who talks *laissez-faire*." Yet he was so alarmed by the growing faith in parental government that he had to express his views. At least he could demonstrate that the party which called itself Liberal was really Tory. At least he could make it clear that in the future the task of genuine Liberalism was to limit the powers of Parliament.

Mallock and the Struggle Against Statism. Spencer was the best-known figure in the ranks of the publicists who defended individualism against its late Victorian enemies. But there were others who, though they lacked Spencer's prestige, were gifted and forceful champions of the cause of self-help. W. H. Mallock, in particular, was respected not only as a novelist and writer on religious subjects but as a propagandist for the ideas of the Liberty and Property Defence League. Impressed with the inadequacies of the literature dealing with social politics, Mallock attempted in a large number of articles, pamphlets, and books to make available, especially to politicians and public speakers, material with which to discredit the advocates of paternalistic government. Nor did he think that there was any time to lose, for he found the speeches and writings of the interventionists filled with wild distortions and mischievous fallacies, and he deplored the ignorance and apathy that made it possible for such errors to circulate. Interventionists, Mallock said in his *Memoirs of Life and Literature,* were "at once wrong and popular, not because they actually invented either the facts or principles proclaimed by them, but because they practised the act of contorting facts into any shape they pleased, no matter what, so long as this amounted to a grimace which was calculated to attract attention, and which, in the absence of any opponents who could counter them by detailed exposure, could, by constant repetition, be invested with the prestige of truth." (*See Document No. 15.*)

As a figure in the history of Victorian social thought, Mallock stands out for several reasons. First, he stressed the importance of statistics in the defense of individualism. Interventionists, to be sure, had long been aware of the potentialities of numbers, and often they used them as their chief and most deadly weapon. Mallock, by becoming expert in the handling of statistics, was able to provide those who shared his convictions with reassuring data: that the poor were not getting poorer, that the middle classes were not disappearing, and that the rich were not getting richer; that the poor were receiving a constantly increasing portion of national wealth, that the classes with moderate means were growing immensely, and that the rich were finding their incomes reduced. Secondly, Mallock viewed it as his mission to teach the converted how to refute, silence, and convert others. He wrote simply, coherently, and always with his audience's needs in view, and he tried constantly to anticipate and answer the objections that his opponents might advance. Small wonder that his *Property and Progress* (1884), *Labour and the Popular Welfare* (1893), *Classes and Masses* (1896), and *Aristocracy and Evolution* (1898) rank high in the literature of individualism. Small wonder, too, that, like Herbert Spencer, he was a hero to those Englishmen who subscribed to the beliefs of the Liberty and Property Defence League and denounced the growth of state power in the age of the great depression.

— 6 —

THE STATE A FRIEND

Champions of the State. While advocates of self-help insisted that the late Victorian government was engaging in too much regulation, defenders of state help complained that it was not intervening enough. Inside and outside Parliament they set forth their ideas on the proper sphere of government. Interventionists often disagreed sharply, but individualists usually lumped them together and dismissed them as Socialists. Some of them were, properly speaking, Socialists, but the vast majority were not only non-Socialists but active anti-Socialists, who saw in the adoption of their programs of state help a sure way of averting the public ownership of the means of production. If anti-Socialist interventionists figured prominently in Parliament, in the churches, in business and farming circles, and in the trade unions, the reason was not that their number was large. Their great advantage was that they felt strongly about their beliefs, and they worked hard to further them. The upshot was that they exercised an influence altogether out of proportion to their numbers.

In the political life of late Victorian England the most important non-Socialist interventionists were Benjamin Disraeli, Lord Randolph Churchill, and Joseph Chamberlain. There were striking differences that divided these three politicians, but these are much less important than the bonds which united them. All three took a positive view of the rôle of the state; all three were critical of the potentialities of self-help. Strong individualists themselves, they had doubts about individualism in the economic sphere. Much more than Disraeli, however, Churchill and Chamberlain turned out to be politicians of the kind that had worried Walter Bagehot when he brought out in 1872 a new introduction to his already standard study of *The English Constitution*—politicians who raised questions that excited what Bagehot called "the lower orders of mankind."

Progressive Toryism. Long before Disraeli began his great ministry of 1874-1880, he had actively defended the cause of progressive Toryism. In speeches, tracts, and such novels as *Coningsby* (1844) and *Sybil* (1845), he had condemned the kind of conservatism that was nothing but a program to save what existed until the time came when it had to be abandoned. He accepted change as inevitable; therefore, the question for him became not whether change should be resisted but "whether that change should be carried out in deference to the manners, the customs, the laws, the traditions of the people, or in deference to abstract principles and arbitrary and general doctrines." Since he believed that the goal of political power was to further the social welfare of the masses, he frequently had occasion to condemn individualism as a creed convenient only for those of the rich and the powerful who believed that the purpose of life was "to acquire, to accumulate, to plunder." Disraeli preached the glories of self-sacrifice—especially of the sort that would reduce the gap that separated the rich and the poor, the two nations "between whom there is no intercourse and sympathy; who are as ignorant of each other's habits, thoughts, and feelings, as if they were dwellers in different zones, or inhabitants of different planets; who are formed by a different breeding, are fed by a different food, are ordered by different manners, and are not governed by the same laws."

A New Feudalism. For an understanding of Disraeli's conception of Toryism, nothing is more important than his view of medieval feudalism, "the ablest, the grandest, the most magnificent and benevolent [principle] that was ever conceived by sage, or ever practised by patriot." Disraeli was impressed not so much by the rights and privileges that feudal institutions permitted as by the obligations, responsibilities, and duties they required. Like so many intellectuals of his time, he idealized feudalism to an extent that would have made it unrecognizable to medieval lords. For all that, his constant plea was that the nineteenth-century counterparts of the old feudal aristocrats should follow the example of their enlightened predecessors. They should recognize and carry out their obligation to care for the underprivileged and the unprivileged. They should keep in mind that when "the Conqueror carved out parts of the land, and introduced the feudal system, he said to the recipient: 'You shall have that estate, but you shall do something for it: you shall feed the poor; you shall endow the Church; you shall defend the land in case of war; and you shall execute justice and maintain truth to the poor for nothing.'" Disraeli's model aristocrat was someone like Lord Henry Sydney, a character in one of his novels, who "devoted his time and thought, labour and life, to one vast and noble purpose, the elevation of the condition of the great body of the people."

In 1872 Disraeli made two speeches that were to play an important part in the great Conservative victory of 1874. The first, delivered in the Free-Trade Hall in Manchester, was received, as the *Times* put it, "amid boundless enthusiasm, and with a running chorus of cheers— of sustained cheers, continued cheers, prolonged cheers.

and renewed cheers, almost exhausting the descriptive vocabulary of reporting." It was this speech that provided the Conservatives with an invaluable slogan. Disraeli told his audience about the theory that there was a great mistake in the Latin translation of the Bible, that instead of "Vanity of vanities, all is vanity," the passage should read, *"Sanitas sanitatum, omnia sanitas."* Disraeli added: "Gentlemen, it is impossible to overrate the importance of the subject. After all, the first consideration of a Minister should be the health of the people." (*See Document No. 16.*)

Disraeli's political opponents seized on his Manchester speech and ridiculed it as a statement of a policy of sewage. In an address delivered at the Crystal Palace in June, 1872, he made it clear that he gloried in such a policy. "It involves," he said, "the state of the dwellings of the people, the moral consequences of which are not less considerable than the physical. It involves their enjoyment of some of the chief elements of nature—air, light, and water. It involves the regulation of their industry, the inspection of their toil. It involves the purity of their provisions, and it touches upon all the means by which you may wean them from habits of excess and of brutality."

That Disraeli's views were not simply campaign promises became clear during the course of his ministry when such measures of social reform were passed as the Public Health Act, the Sale of Food and Drugs Act, the Employers' and Workmen's Act, the Artisans' Dwellings Act, and the Merchant Shipping Act. If these accomplishments fell short of Disraeli's ideals, there are several explanations. First, Disraeli was old and ill, and this meant that he had only limited energy to devote to his program. Secondly, Anglo-Russian relations deteriorated rapidly during the course of his ministry; in the face of foreign dangers, domestic concerns were pushed to the background. Thirdly, Disraeli had not converted all or even the bulk of the members of his party to his creed. He was still disliked by many of his colleagues, who dismissed him as a foreigner, an opportunist, a demagogue, a visionary, and a fraud. From a long run point of view, however, Disraeli was enormously successful. His ministry did translate some of his principles into legislation, and this was enough to build

up a tradition of Tory Democracy—a tradition that has
kept the Conservative Party not only alive but lively in
the twentieth century. In the prophetic words that the
much-abused Tory poet, Alfred Austin, wrote of Disraeli:

> How poor were Fame, did grief confess
> That death can make a great life less,
>   Or end the help it gave!
> Our wreaths may fade, our flowers may wane,
> But his well-ripened deeds remain,
>   Untouched, above his grave.

Enter Churchill.   Disraeli's most important succes-
sor as a Tory Democrat in late Victorian England was
Lord Randolph Churchill. Elected to the House of Commons in the Conservative landslide of 1874, Churchill
gave no signs during his early parliamentary career of the
rôle he was soon to play in English politics. His attend-
ance was irregular and his interest in public affairs was in-
conspicuous. Only after the fall of the Conservative government in 1880 and the victory of Gladstone's Liberals
did he emerge as a powerful figure on the political scene.
He made his reputation in the course of the prolonged
dispute over the admission (which he opposed) of the
atheist Charles Bradlaugh to his seat in the House of
Commons. Playing the part of David in opposition to
Gladstone's Goliath, Churchill rapidly achieved fame
throughout the country and heroic stature within his
party. His treatment of the Grand Old Man delighted
Conservatives and infuriated Liberals. With the utmost
earnestness he would blame Gladstone for the decline of
religion, the disintegration of the Empire, the waning of
commerce, the decay of industry, the emigration of labor,
military defeats, the lowering of national prestige, and the
appearance in a once peaceful country of "the spectres of
revolution and of communism." When Churchill was in a
less solemn mood, he would strike out at Gladstone with
words like these: "Gentlemen, we live in an age of advertisement, the age of Holloway's pills, of Colman's mus-
tard, and of Horniman's pure tea. . . . The Prime Minister is the greatest living master of the art of personal
political advertisement. Holloway, Colman, and Horniman are nothing compared with him. Every act of his,

whether it be for the purposes of health, or of recreation, or of religious devotion, is spread before the eyes of every man, woman, and child in the United Kingdom on large and glaring placards. . . . For the purposes of recreation he has selected the felling of trees, and we may usefully remark that his amusements, like his politics, are essentially destructive. Every afternoon the whole world is invited to assist at the crashing fall of some beech or elm or oak. The forest laments in order that Mr. Gladstone may perspire, and full accounts of these proceedings are forwarded by special correspondents to every daily paper every recurring morning."

Trust the People. To tease and to embarrass Gladstone was not enough of a policy if the Conservatives were to regain power. Churchill was impressed by the electoral defeat his party had suffered in 1880, and he became increasingly convinced that future victories would depend on a rejuvenation of Toryism. So it was that he came to defend ideas that sounded very much like Disraeli's. (*See Document No. 17.*) So it was that he took an active part in the organization of the Primrose League, the purpose of which was to perpetuate the memory of Disraeli and what he stood for. In Churchill's words: "The maintenance of an ancient monarchy, the consolidation of an unequalled empire, the preservation of national morality by the connection of the State with a pure religion, the vigilant guardianship of popular rights already secured, the timely extension of those rights as the diffusion of knowledge and the progress of society may demand, the vigorous and earnest promotion of every social reform which can in any degree raise the character and condition of the English people—these are the objects of the Primrose League." The masses, Churchill insisted, must get rid of their unsound views of the nature of the Conservative Party. They must be made to see it as the party not of the privileged but of the masses. It had no fear of democracy, it accepted the motto, "Trust the People," and it worked for social progress. Like Tennyson, Churchill believed the true Conservative to be the person who "lops the moulder'd branch away."

The Fall of Churchill. Disraeli was able to put some of his ideas into practice, but Churchill hardly had a chance to do so. Named Chancellor of the Exchequer by Lord Salisbury in 1886, he seemed to have arrived. But he quickly became involved in a dispute over the budget—a dispute that centered on his fiscal policy of reducing government expenditures and shifting the burden of taxation to the wealthy. The upshot was that he resigned from the ministry. A member of Parliament until his tragically early death in 1895, he became more and more radical in his social and economic views, but after his resignation he lost all importance as a political leader. The members of his party were delighted with him as long as they were out of office. He was a splendid speaker, he had what Matthew Arnold called "freshness and go," he attracted a great deal of publicity, and he could win the votes of the working classes. Once his colleagues were in power, however, they cast him aside. They disliked him as a personality, finding him difficult, reckless, eccentric, impudent, and insolent. They put up with his unattractive traits as long as Gladstone and his fellow-Liberals were the enemies, but as soon as a Conservative ministry seemed secure, things were different.

It was not only Churchill's personality that alienated his colleagues; it was also his program. Like Disraeli, he had not succeeded in educating his party. He had supporters throughout the country, but many of his parliamentary colleagues were alarmed by the implications of Tory Democracy. They viewed it as "the wolf of Radicalism in the sheep-skin of Toryism." Oscar Wilde had Mrs. Erlynne say in *Lady Windermere's Fan* (1892) that it was so important nowadays to think like a Tory and talk like a Radical. Churchill's trouble was that he both thought and talked like a Radical. He himself recognized that it was one thing to win applause at mass meetings; it was quite another to gain support in the House of Commons for a legislative program.

Five years after his resignation from the cabinet Churchill sent to his wife one of the most pathetic letters ever written by a disillusioned politician. "I have waited with great patience for the tide to turn," he said, "but it has not turned, and will not now turn in time. . . . All confirms me in my decision to have done with politics, and try to make a little money for the boys and ourselves.

. . . More than two-thirds in all probability of my life is over, and I will not spend the remainder of my years in beating my head against a stone-wall. . . . I am quite tired and dead-sick of it all, and will not continue political life any longer." Events proved that Churchill's pessimism over the fate of Tory Democracy was excessive. The Conservatives did not legislate as much as Churchill would have liked, but in the nineties they did pass enough social welfare legislation to demonstrate that Churchill was more successful than he knew. Even Lord Salisbury—certainly no Tory Democrat—insisted in 1895 that "we have got, as far as we can, to make this country more pleasant to live in for the vast majority of those who live in it." Lord Randolph's pessimism proved to be overdone for another reason. He died too soon to be able to gauge the abilities of his son Winston as a champion of Tory Democracy.

Property and Ransom. Along with Disraeli and Churchill, Joseph Chamberlain bulked large as an interventionist in late Victorian England. An extraordinarily gifted businessman, Chamberlain amassed a fortune in the years before the great depression began. When he reached his late thirties, he was able to retire from his screw-manufacturing firm to devote full time to the public service. Convinced that much of human misery was both curable and preventable, he singled out ignorance and inadequate housing as the social abuses that in an immediate sense most needed to be combated, and he proceeded to attack them. The result was that he rapidly emerged as the most creative and imaginative municipal administrator and reformer of his time. Elected mayor of Birmingham in 1873, he made it clear that he believed in a do-much government—one that would work for better public health, housing, and education. In 1876, after having established an international reputation for his local activities, he was elected to represent Birmingham in the House of Commons. A member of the radical wing of the Liberal Party, he played an important part in the electoral victory of the Liberals in 1880. The Grand Young Man was rewarded with the post of President of the Board of Trade in Gladstone's second ministry.

Just as Lord Randolph Churchill alarmed his fellow

Conservatives, so Chamberlain alarmed his Liberal colleagues, for he urged the active intervention of the state in areas which many of the members of his party felt had better be left to individual enterprise. He made one speech in particular that created a sensation not only in England but in many parts of the world. This was an address on "Work for the New Parliament," which he delivered in Birmingham in January, 1885. Confessing that, as a member of the radical wing of a Liberal government, he had sometimes found it hard to reconcile his loyalty to his party with his loyalty to the principles he was supposed to represent, he proceeded to restate some of these principles. Certain that domestic legislation was going to be more and more concerned with social subjects, he proclaimed the main problem of the future to be the promotion of the greater happiness of the masses. Time was, he said, when every Englishman was born "with natural rights, with a right to a share in the great inheritance of the community, with a right to a part of the land of his birth." For a variety of reasons these rights had been lost, and private ownership had won out, achieving the sanction of law and the protection of custom. And so, Chamberlain asked: "What ransom will property pay for the security which it enjoys! What substitute will it find for the natural rights which have ceased to be recognized? Society is banded together in order to protect itself against the instincts of those of its members who would make very short work of private ownership if they were left alone. That is all very well, but I maintain that society owes to these men something more than mere toleration in return for the restrictions which it places upon their liberty of action." Chamberlain's point was that the defenders of property should stop talking so much about their rights and start to recognize their obligations and responsibilities. For an age was getting under way that would witness many attempts "to lessen the evils which poverty brings in its train, to increase the rewards of labour, to bring hope to the miserable, to give courage to the weak, and in this way to advance the aim and end of all our Liberal policy—the greatest happiness of the greatest number." (*See Document No. 18.*)

Chamberlain's ardent belief in intervention aroused

widespread fears among many of his colleagues, who longed for a return to "the era B. C." (Before Chamberlain). They had no desire to see the Liberal Party made into a working-class organization, a Labour Party. Small wonder that they rejoiced that the Grand Young Man was so opposed to Gladstone's scheme of home rule for Ireland that in 1886 he withdrew from the Liberal Party to form an independent group, the Liberal Unionists. This new party coöperated with the Conservatives to defeat home rule for Ireland, and by 1895 Chamberlain himself accepted the office of Secretary of State for the Colonies in a Conservative ministry headed by Lord Salisbury. There he was working with the party that Disraeli and Churchill had tried to educate in the ways of Tory Democracy.

After the great disruption of 1886 Chamberlain continued to be interested in social reform, but other objectives seemed even more pressing—maintaining the Union with Ireland, improving imperial relations, stemming the inroads of foreign competition, and reversing the policy of free trade. As Chamberlain acknowledged in a number of public speeches, the Liberal who "places the Union first of all is bound to make some sacrifices for what will be his paramount object. He is bound to make some sacrifices of extreme views. He is bound to put aside for a time some of his cherished ambitions. This is an elementary condition of all combinations whatsoever." The upshot was that, as a social reformer, Chamberlain never attained on a national scale the success he had achieved in Birmingham. Like Disraeli and Churchill, however, he helped to alter the late Victorian environment by spreading the idea that the state was the Englishman's friend, not his enemy.

Pledged by the Bible. This view of the state was also furthered by clergymen in all the leading churches. The late Victorian period was a time when traditional religious beliefs were being transformed by Biblical criticism and Darwinian science; when such outstanding writers as Swinburne, Hardy, Butler, and Meredith, if not Browning, rejected Christianity; when Charles Bradlaugh, Mrs. Annie Besant and their followers were preaching atheism to the working classes; when Leslie

Stephen and Thomas Henry Huxley were urging agnosticism on the middle classes; and when Mrs. Humphry
Ward's novel on agnosticism, *Robert Elsmere* (1888),
caused an almost unbelievable stir. In this setting, clergymen of all denominations concerned themselves with what
the eminent Cambridge textual critic and Bishop of
Durham, Brooke Westcott, liked to call "the social
aspects of Christianity." They emphasized that their
particular church had not only a spiritual but a social
mission, and that they were "pledged by every page of
the Testament, Old and New, to fight the battle of the
poor." They preached to the rich of their responsibilities,
they insisted repeatedly that, if Christ were to come again,
He would be found living not with the wealthy in Park
Lane but with the downtrodden in West Ham, and they
renounced the idea of a do-little state. It was under-
standable, therefore, that individualists often complained
that "vaguely benevolent aspirations after world-bettering
find a natural and prolific seed-bed in the minds of the
younger clergy who see of course a great deal of misery,
and have not learnt that short cuts to prosperity only too
often lead to most calamitous endings."

   Salvationists and the Battle of the Poor.   It was not
only younger clergymen who denounced *laissez-faire;*
some of the best-known senior clergy in late Victorian
England condemned it, too. Outstanding among them was
William Booth, founder and first general of the Salvation
Army, who once told Rudyard Kipling that if he thought
he could win *"one* more soul to the Lord" by walking on
his head and playing his tambourine with his toes, he
would learn how. Booth had nothing but scorn for "those
anti-Christian economists who hold that it is an offence
against the doctrine of the survival of the fittest to try to
save the weakest from going to the wall, and who believe
that once a man is down the supreme duty of a self-
regarding Society is to jump upon him." According to
Booth, the idea of *laissez-faire* and the laws of supply
and demand were simply "excuses by which those who
stand on firm ground salve their consciences when they
leave their brother to sink." If Christianity was to stop
being a "mockery to perishing men," he insisted that
something would have to be done to extirpate poverty an ¹

to regenerate the lower strata of society. Booth, to be sure, had numerous enemies who dismissed him as a char-latan, plagiarist, and fanatic and who quipped that Barnum forgot Booth when he called himself the greatest showman on earth. But even those who detested "Pope Booth" and his tambourines, drums, processions, and medicine-man methods recognized the force with which he dramatized the war against poverty and the energy with which he popularized Christianity as a religion hold-ing out hope to the lowest elements in society.

General Booth had his counterpart among Anglicans, Methodists, Presbyterians, Congregationalists, and Roman Catholics. In every English church there were leading clergymen who agreed with the words of that Mosaic Radical, Cardinal Manning: "If the great end of life were to multiply yards of cloth and cotton twist, and if the glory of England consists or consisted in multiplying without stint or limit these articles and the like at the lowest possible price so as to undersell all the nations of the world, well, then, let us go on. But if the domestic life of the people be vital above all; if the peace, the purity of homes, the education of children, the duties of wives and mothers, the duties of husbands and of fathers, be written in the natural law of mankind, and if these things are sacred, far beyond anything that can be sold in the market, then I say, if the hours of labour result-ing from the unregulated sale of a man's strength and skill shall lead to the destruction of domestic life, to the neglect of children, to turning wives and mothers into living machines, and of fathers and husbands into—what shall I say, creatures of burden?—I will not use any other word—who rise before the sun, and come back when it is set, wearied and able only to take food and lie down to rest; the domestic life of men exists no longer, and we dare not go in this path." Indeed, one of the main reasons religion in late Victorian England survived so successfully the onslaughts of Darwinism and Biblical criticism was that clergymen demonstrated their aware-ness that the spiritual and social welfare of their parish-ioners were inseparable. Some even insisted that the minister who hoped to further the cause of religion had 'o begin by preaching social reform. Sartorius, the slum landlord in Shaw's first play, *Widowers' Houses* (1892), shouted that he was an Englishman and that he would permit no clerical interference in his business. But the times were against him.

The Humanitarians. Apart from politicians and clergymen, there were other articulate interventionists in late Victorian England: farmers, landowners, and businessmen who wanted tariff reform; trade unionists who called for state help to combat unemployment and to introduce an eight-hour day; and middle and upper-class humanitarians who could have said with the clergyman William Tuckwell: "The misery which I encountered haunted me with a sense of guilt; I was ill at ease and self-reproachful unless when labouring to remove it." These humanitarians were often moved to action by their conception of religion; they felt, like Lord Brabazon, the need "to apply to the social sores of our time (irritated and inflamed by the poison of class ignorance and prejudice) the healing remedies of personal ministration and Christian sympathy." Often, too, they were influenced and fortified by the criticisms of *laissez-faire* set forth in such seminal works as Thomas Carlyle's *Chartism* (1840), *Past and Present* (1843), and *Latter-Day Pamphlets* (1850), John Ruskin's *Unto This Last* (1862), *Fors Clavigera* (1871-84), and *Munera Pulveris* (1872), John Stuart Mill's revisions of his *Principles of Political Economy* (1848) and his *Autobiography* (1873), and T. H. Green's posthumously published *Works* (1885-88), especially his *Lectures on the Principles of Political Obligation*.

In the ranks of these late Victorian humanitarians, journalists like William T. Stead often figured prominently; and what gave them importance was the growth of literacy, the extension of the suffrage, and the long duration of the depression. Indeed, the social reformer, W. Walker Stephens, was not only a flatterer but a wise man when he dedicated a book to the British newspaper press "without whose aid no improvement in social conditions can be introduced or carried out." In view of the ardor with which interventionists in the age of the great depression urged the abandonment of what Lord Brabazon called "superstitious worship of the doctrine of *laissez-faire,"* it was no surprise that Herbert Spencer felt depressed about the future and that members of the Liberty and Property Defence League found their task both urgent and overwhelming. Oscar Wilde knew what he was about when he had a character in *An Ideal Husband* (1895) say: "Oh, damn sympathy. There is a great deal too much of that sort of thing going on nowadays."

— 7 —

SOCIALIST DISSENSION

The Socialist Panacea. To end the depression and to assure economic progress, individualists believed it vital for the government to avoid meddling in economic affairs. Interventionists found it imperative for the government to pass particular kinds of legislation. But there were some interventionists who were Socialists. They believed that to end the depression and to guarantee economic progress it was necessary to get rid of private ownership of the basic means of production. In the words of the small group of Socialists who, in 1894, brought out the minority report of the Royal Commission on Labour: "the whole force of democratic statesmanship must, in our opinion, henceforth be directed to the substitution, as fast as possible, of public for capitalist enterprise."

A Handful of Socialists. Already in the Germany of the late seventies, Socialists—to the horror of Bismarck—were polling an impressive vote and sending representatives to the Reichstag, but in England Socialists were almost non-existent in the early years of the great depression. As late as 1881 John Morley, the Liberal politician and historian, remarked in his biography of *Richard Cobden* that socialism was much less discussed in England than in any other European country. About the same time Prince Kropotkin discovered that his English lectures on socialism were drawing absurdly small audiences. When Karl Marx, after a long exile in England, died in 1883, the event went almost unnoticed among the people he had expected to lead the Socialist revolution. By the time the great depression ended in the late nineties, English Socialists were still strikingly few in number. Again, however, as so often in history, statistics are deceptive, for the Socialists, though few, were energetic and generous with time and money; and they inspired almost unbelievable fears among the late Victorians. This was not only because they denounced the principle of private property; it was also because they were viewed—sometimes correctly and more often incorrectly—as atheists and advocates of violence. In the words that Tennyson had the Socialist villain speak in his play, *The Promise of May* (1882):

> The storm is hard at hand will sweep away
> Thrones, churches, ranks, traditions, customs, marriage,
> One of the feeblest!

Post-Victorians know, of course, that no revolution took place in late Victorian England, but the late Victorians did not have this knowledge; if they had had it, they probably would not have believed it. It was no accident that the first of George Gissing's books to attract public interest was *Demos* (1886), a novel critical of socialism.

The label Socialist was often loosely used in the late nineteenth century. Lord Randolph Churchill and Joseph Chamberlain, for example, were frequently denounced as Socialists—even though they viewed the reforms they proposed as measures to stave off public ownership of the means of production. When the Liberal leader, Sir William Harcourt, made his frequently quoted statement in the early nineties that "we are all Socialists now," and when the Prince of Wales made a similar comment, neither meant that the English people favored public ownership. Some of the Socialists themselves added to the confusion by calling socialistic practically any measure of state intervention in social and economic life. The Fabian leader, Sidney Webb, was notorious for doing this. On at least one occasion, after pointing to factory acts, income taxes, public education, and legislation for improved dwellings as evidence of the progress of socialism in England, he added self-consciously: "Philanthropic reformers will be surprised to find some of these measures classed as socialistic."

Many groups of Socialists were formed in the late Victorian era. Some were strictly local societies that most contemporaries never heard of. Some—the Guild of St. Matthew and the Christian Social Union—were mainly religious organizations which considered the future of Christianity intimately linked with that of socialism and which in the spirit of Charles Kingsley sought to dispel the idea that the Bible was a weapon to keep the masses in their place. James Mavor Morell in Shaw's *Candida* (1895) was an Anglican clergyman and a Christian Socialist, who participated actively in the affairs of the Guild of St. Matthew and the Christian Social Union. Finally, some of the Socialist groups were national secular organizations which sometimes had an overlapping membership.

A Curse of Quarreling. Probably the distinguishing characteristic of the national groups—the Social Democratic Federation, the Socialist League, the Fabian Society, and the Independent Labour Party—was the hostility that the members of each organization felt toward the members of the others and often toward one another. It is perhaps not difficult to understand this lack of fraternity. At a time when socialism was so unrespectable in England, the people attracted by it tended to be erratic and difficult personalities, who prided themselves on being different and original; and such people do not make for a harmonious group. On occasion the Socialists coöperated, but their inability to unite seriously lessened their effectiveness. Sidney Webb issued a masterpiece of understatement when he wrote of English socialism in the 1880's: "It need hardly be said that petty jealousies and personal quarrels have not been wanting in this as in every other popular movement, and its organisation has constantly suffered from these causes." William Morris was far more accurate when he said that "there seems to be a sort of curse of quarreling upon us," and when he added the lament that Socialists "will make things hard for their comrades." If anti-Socialists knew how temperamental and quarrelsome the Socialists were, they would never have feared them as they did. There would have been fewer people like the Duchess of Berwick in Oscar Wilde's *Lady Windermere's Fan* (1892) who worried about living in "these dreadful socialistic days."

Probably no leading late Victorian Socialist was so much of a prima donna as H. M. Hyndman, the wealthy and disillusioned Tory, who played an important part in organizing the Democratic Federation in 1881. On a business trip to the United States Hyndman had read a French translation of the first volume of Marx's *Das Kapital,* and he believed what he read. He set forth his version of Marxism in a short book, *England for All,* in the preface to which he acknowledged his indebtedness to a great and original thinker. He neglected to mention Marx by name, fearing that to do so would hurt the book, for the English, he said, hated foreigners. The upshot was that Hyndman aroused the wrath of Marx and Engels, the first of a long line of fellow-Socialists whom he was to antagonize.

The Federation in Action. At the outset the Democratic Federation had as its objectives the direct representation of labor in Parliament and social reform, and its early program stressed the improvement of Anglo-Irish relations and the relief of agricultural distress by means of land nationalization. By 1883, after many early members had withdrawn, Hyndman converted the organization into a distinctly Socialist group, which demanded the nationalization not only of the land but of all the means of production, exchange, and distribution; the next year the name of the organization was changed to the Social Democratic Federation. Its members—never even a thousand who paid dues in the eighties—accepted by and large the teachings of Marx. They believed that labor was the source of all value, that since labor did not receive all that it produced it was exploited, that as time went by the ownership of the means of production would be vested in the hands of fewer and fewer capitalists, and that the workers, suffering from increasing misery, would deprive their exploiters of the ownership of the means of production. The members of the Federation preached these doctrines in speeches, debates, books, pamphlets, and their newspaper *Justice;* and they exploited the unemployment problem and took advantage of strikes in order to gain publicity for their organization. Already in 1884, Herbert Spencer testified to the success of their propaganda by taking note of Hyndman and the Federation in *The Man versus the State.*

The most distinguished member of the Federation, William Morris, had already won an international reputation as a poet and artist when he joined it in 1883. Many of his contemporaries were shocked by his conversion. Tennyson was convinced that he had "gone crazy," and the young novelist, George Gissing, feared that Morris would "inevitably coarsen himself in the company of ruffians." But for years Morris had been looking for such an organization. Obsessed with the meanness, ugliness, and cruelty of what he liked to call his "accursed age," he gradually lost faith in the power of the Liberal Party to do good. In a revealing letter to a close friend, Morris wrote on New Year's Day, 1881: "I have of late been somewhat melancholy (rather too strong a word, but I don't know another), not so much so as not to enjoy life in a way, but just so much as a man of middle age who has met with rubs (though less than his share of them) may sometimes be allowed to be. When one is just so much subdued one is apt to turn more specially from thinking of one's own affairs to more worthy matters; and my mind is very full of the great change which I hope is slowly coming over the world, and of which surely this new year will be one of the landmarks." In particular he expressed the hope that 1881 would "do a good turn of work toward the abasement of the rich and the raising up of the poor, which is of all things most to be longed for, till people can at last rub out from their dictionaries altogether these dreadful words rich and poor. . . ."

Morris gave a vast amount of time, energy, and money to the Federation. He studied the writings of Marx and other Socialists, and he worried that he did not know German and that he handled statistics inadequately. At a time when Walter Pater was urging the value of beauty for its own sake, Morris lectured and wrote on socialism in an effort to win converts to the cause. He urged Algernon Swinburne, his republican friend, to join the Federation and write for it some stirring poems that could be set to music and sung at meetings of the faithful; and if Dante Gabriel Rossetti had still been alive, Morris would doubtless have tried to persuade even that poet's poet to write some ballads and sonnets for the Socialists.

By the end of 1884 Morris was unhappy about the Federation. Along with Marx's daughter, Eleanor, and her lover, Edward Aveling, and others, he withdrew to form a new organization, rejoicing that he would not have to shake hands with Hyndman again. For his part Hyndman blamed the split on his opposition to the illicit relationship between Aveling and Eleanor Marx; he wanted them to marry. Morris attributed the schism to Hyndman's dictatorial leanings, his opportunism, his intrigues and conspiracies, and his theatrical boasts and warnings of immediate violent revolution. Morris detested Hyndman's wild talk and his policy of using the Federation as a bogey to terrify the government. He considered this dangerous, for eventually people would find out that the Federation was "a small party without organization and with no very clear aims." Worse still, they would discover that the Federation had been unable to win the support of the working classes, nearly all of whom believed in capitalism and class coöperation.

The Socialist League. As Morris and some of the other secessionists viewed it, the main purpose of the new society, the Socialist League, was educational. Depression and the relative decline of the English economic position were signs that capitalism was weakening and that the way was being prepared for socialism. Since it was likely that the English would be the first people to achieve socialism, it was urgent to educate the masses for what lay ahead. To "make Socialists," members of the League gave lectures and published pamphlets, books, and

a newspaper, *Commonweal,* easily the most literary Socialist newspaper of the nineteenth century. (*See Document No. 19.*) Morris himself was almost unbelievably
active as a professional agitator. "The ideas which have
taken hold of me," he confessed to a friend, "will not let
me rest: nor can I see anything else worth thinking of."
Despite gout and sciatica, he lectured and wrote constantly about his love of art and his hatred of modern
civilization. He argued that art was handcuffed as long
as capitalism existed and that there was neither a present
nor a future for popular art until the gap between the
rich and the poor was eliminated. He constantly expressed his sense of guilt about the contrast between his
happy working hours and the monotonous toil to which
he considered most of his contemporaries condemned.

For all the efforts of Morris and his colleagues, the
League did not flourish. Money troubles were endless,
converts few, and internal conflicts intense. In letters to
his friends and family, Morris often spoke of his "low
spirits about the prospects of our 'party,' if I can dignify
a little knot of men by such a word." Soon the clashes
became unendurable. A group that was impatient with the
educational aims of the League and insisted on the need
for immediate parliamentary action withdrew. Morris
found himself in a League quite different from what he
had intended. For anarchists were now in control—people
who went about the streets urging the use of dynamite
and calling for an uprising. As far as Morris was concerned, revolution was "about as likely to happen in our
time as the conversion of Englishmen from stupidity to
quick-wittedness." In 1890, the year his masterpiece of
a Socialist utopia, *News from Nowhere,* appeared as a
series of articles in *Commonweal,* he resigned from the
League. For lack of financial backing, the anarchists were
soon forced to disband.

The Fabian Society. Compared with the Socialist
League and the Social Democratic Federation, the Fabian
Society was a relatively homogeneous body with clear
aims acceptable to the bulk of its members. It began as an
offshoot from the Fellowship of the New Life, an ethical
Socialist group founded in London in 1883. Inspired by
Thomas Davidson, an enthusiastic Scottish philosopher,

the Fellowship had as its aim the "reconstruction of Society in accordance with the highest moral possibilities." Each member was to subordinate material to spiritual things and seek to cultivate a perfect character. In January, 1884, some of the Davidsonian Fellows set up a separate organization, the Fabian Society. The Fellowship, with its primarily spiritual aims, continued to exist until 1898, emphasizing character development, ethical socialism, and the simple life. The new organization, the Fabian Society, stressed the present more than the future and society more than the individual. With a view to furthering social reconstruction, the Fabians were to hold meetings, attend sessions of other groups, and secure information about "all contemporary social movements and social needs." Within a few months the Society issued its first tract, *Why Are the Many Poor?*, on the title page of which appeared the motto that explained the organization's name: "For the right moment you must wait, as Fabius did most patiently, when warring against Hannibal, though many censured his delays; but when the time comes you must strike hard, as Fabius did, or your waiting will be in vain, and fruitless." Since Fabius never did strike hard, the members of the Society were frequently taunted about their ignorance of ancient history. Furthermore, though they planned to reconstruct society, they were uncertain as to how to go about doing it.

Among the early Fabians were anarchists, insurrectionists, students of psychical research, and marriageable young women who, when they succeeded in their husband-hunting, proceeded, as Shaw said, to drop out. Among them, too, was Edith Nesbit, who disrupted meetings with her constant fainting and who gave few signs of the talent she was to develop as a writer of children's stories permeated with Socialist propaganda. Like the other Socialist organizations, the Fabian Society was not free from what Shaw called "considerable strife of temperaments." What saved it in its first years and kept it from remaining an obscure drawing-room society was the presence in its ranks of a number of exceptionally bright young men and women who worked tirelessly in its behalf: irreverent George Bernard Shaw, then an unpublishable novelist and a budding critic who wrote witty

Fabian tracts; Mrs. Annie Besant, atheist, advocate of birth control, probably the most gifted orator of the time, and the best-known figure among the early Fabians; Sidney Webb, the civil servant who loved to deal with statistics and to draw up reports and who had the opportunity to lavish this love on such early Fabian tracts as *Facts for Socialists* (1887), *Facts for Londoners* (1889), and *Figures for Londoners* (1889); and a few others.

In 1887 the Society adopted its revised "Basis," which proclaimed its faith in socialism and the need to spread this faith. (*See Document No. 20.*) Two years later, when the Society had about 150 members, the *Fabian Essays in Socialism* appeared. Edward R. Pease, a charter member and an early secretary of the Society, has said of this book (based on a series of lectures given by the leaders of the Society) that it "presented the case for Socialism in plain language which everybody could understand. It based Socialism, not on the speculations of a German philosopher, but on the obvious evolution of society as we see it around us. It accepted economic science as taught by the accredited British professors; it built up the edifice of Socialism on the foundations of our existing political and social institutions: it proved that Socialism was but the next step in the development of society, rendered inevitable by the changes which followed from the industrial revolution of the eighteenth century." For a book on socialism, it sold extremely well. Nevertheless, it is often so dull that it is hard to understand how those who listened to the original lectures ever managed to stay awake.

The importance of the Fabians on the late Victorian scene has constantly been exaggerated. Certainly they tried to permeate all kinds of organizations, political, educational, and social, with their socialism. With their numerous tracts, they doubtless came to serve as a bureau of information and statistics. And by stressing gradualism they probably helped to make socialism a somewhat less terrifying word than it had been. Nevertheless, the conclusion seems inescapable that the leaders of the Fabians were experts in advertising who knew how important it was constantly to announce how successful they were in their activities. Even modern scholars have taken them at their word and made them appear more influential than they really were among the late Victorians.

An Appeal to John Smith. The presence in the *Fabian Essays* of two pieces by Shaw has helped to keep the volume in circulation. Back in the nineties, however, it never approached the popularity of *Merrie England* (1894), a remarkable little book written by the Manchester journalist, Robert Blatchford. Like so many late Victorian Socialists, Blatchford was shaped by his reading of Carlyle, Ruskin, Mill, and Henry George, on all of whom he drew for the *Clarion* articles that he reprinted in book form with the title *Merrie England*. Despite signs of hasty composition and what Blatchford called "the bitter hostility and prejudice with which socialist books are commonly received," the volume caught on and sold a phenomenal number of copies. Its success was due to its skilful mingling of socialism with patriotism, moralistic outbursts, denunciations of materialism, and appeals to Christ. Its success was also due to its clear, direct, and homely prose; it was written in the form of personal letters to a typical worker, Mr. John Smith.

Blatchford's aims were to explain to Mr. Smith the meaning of socialism, to rid him of any prejudices that he had against it, and to answer any objections that he raised. Blatchford condemned capitalism as a curse, competition as wasteful, cruel, and wrong, and the factory system as ugly, disagreeable, mechanical, injurious to health, unnecessary, and dangerous to national existence. His thesis was that if the labor of the people were wisely organized and applied, there would be abundance and above all leisure for everybody; but, as long as capitalism existed, the country would suffer from low wages, long working hours, unemployment, insecurity, low standards of public health and morality, pauperism, crime, and false ideals. Convinced that capitalism would collapse, Blatchford considered himself a recruiting sergeant for socialism. Unlike many of his fellow-Socialists who talked as if socialism were either just around the corner or already established, he was forthright enough to recognize that it was in its infancy and that Socialists were few in number and generally unpopular. Nor did Blatchford pretend that socialism and heaven would be the same thing. He argued simply that socialism, though far from being a perfect way of life, would be a "very great improvement upon the system under which we now live." (*See Document No. 21.*)

Blatchford ended *Merrie England* with a plea for labor representation in Parliament. Both Liberals and Tories, he complained, were committed to the preservation of capitalism; hence, they were of no use to workers. (*See Document No. 22.*) Nor were trade unions alone sufficient to secure labor's rights. Therefore, he urged John Smith to erase the words Liberal and Tory from his vocabulary, form his own party, and return only labor representatives to Parliament. As Blatchford put it to John Smith: "You never elect an employer as president of a Trades Council; or as chairman of a Trade Union Congress; or as a member of a Trade Union. You never ask an employer to lead you during a strike. But at election times, when you ought to stand by your class, the whole body of Trade Union workers turn into black-legs, and fight for the Capitalist and against the workers."

The Independent Labour Party. Blatchford pleaded with workers to back the recently founded national Independent Labour Party, among whose leaders were Blatchford himself and, above all, Keir Hardie, the Scottish trade unionist, spokesman in Parliament for the unemployed, and champion of socialism as Christian economics. At the foundation conference of the party in Bradford in 1893, some of those present wanted the new organization to be called the Socialist Labour Party, but this proposal was voted down for fear that such a name would frighten away many trade unionists. While the Independent Labour Party was not Socialist in name, it was Socialist in program, for it favored public ownership of the means of production, distribution, and exchange; and its founders hoped that it would be as successful in furthering the demands of labor as its model, the independent party of Irish Nationalists, had been in securing Irish reforms. Although the majority of voters consisted of working-class people, these hopes were not realized. Hardie's party did not catch on. Trade union members and workers in general continued to vote either for Liberal or Conservative candidates; the Social Democratic

Federation not only did not coöperate but condemned the Independent Labour Party; the London Fabians were critical of it; and the leaders of the party—most notably Hardie and Blatchford—did not get on well together. In short, the party failed in its attempt to attain parliamentary power by uniting Socialists and trade unionists. Hardie himself lost his seat in the House of Commons in the election of 1895, and not a single member of the party was returned.

The Labour Representation Committee. Negotiations to achieve unity between the Socialist organizations and the trade unions did continue sporadically, and in 1900—in the midst of the Boer War—the Labour Representation Committee was set up by representatives from the Independent Labour Party, the Social Democratic Federation, the Fabian Society, and the trade unions. Because of the war, the Committee was barely noticed, and expectations were that it would fail. What saved it was the fear that trade unionists had of the union-smashing intentions of their employers. The great depression, with its low profits, had encouraged many English employers to look with envy on their American competitors who rarely had unions with which to contend. Though by the turn of the century prices and profits were slowly mounting, employers continued to favor restrictions on unions. Like their American counterparts, English businessmen turned to the courts to attain their objective, and they rejoiced when the famous Taff Vale decision was handed down in 1901, for it made a union liable for damages caused by its members during a strike. The importance of the Taff Vale case cannot be exaggerated, for it encouraged many of the trade unions to rally to the support of the Labour Representation Committee.

These trade unions, however, had a long tradition of voting for the Liberal Party; they were filled with members who praised the virtues that Samuel Smiles, the most famous Victorian author of how-to books, had preached in *Self-Help* (1859), *Character* (1871), *Thrift* (1875), and *Duty* (1880). Therefore, the Socialists on the Committee, few in number and with limited financial resources, were forced to recognize that the new group could not champion socialism. As a result the Social

Democratic Federation soon denounced the Committee; and the Fabians, considering it premature and sure to fail, preferred to permeate the older parties. Only an incurable optimist could have believed that the Committee, renamed in 1906 the Labour Party, would achieve office by 1924 and power by 1945. It seemed far more probable that Nature, as Private Willis sang in *Iolanthe*, would continue to contrive

> That every boy and every gal
>   That's born into the world alive
> [Be] either a little Liberal
>   Or else a little Conservative!

— 8 —

IRISH AGITATION

To Pacify Ireland. English businessmen and farmers who wanted protection against foreign competition, and English workers who wanted social welfare legislation often complained that Parliament in the age of the great depression gave so much of its time to Irish affairs. Parliament did, in fact, devote an incredible number of hours to Irish questions. Column after column in the *Parliamentary Debates* testifies to the length and passion of a discussion that was intimately bound up with the impact of the great depression.

Some years before the onset of the depression, Gladstone, beginning his first ministry, announced that his mission was to pacify Ireland. His decision to undertake this mission in 1868 came as a response to the activities of the notorious Fenians. These champions of Irish independence believed in the efficacy of dynamite and armed insurrection. Scattered all over the world but especially violent in the United States, they did their best to embarrass and discredit the English government. Their hatred of the English was boundless, and they blamed their enemies for everything that went wrong in Irish affairs, including, of course, the unspeakably horrible famine of the late forties. To Gladstone the behavior of the Fenians was especially painful. Highly patriotic, he was ashamed that his country, which had defended the freedom of Greeks, Magyars, Italians, and other subject nationalities, should be held up by the Fenians as the prime example of an oppressor. More than that, he recognized that the Irish had certain legitimate grievances; his reading of history had convinced him that they had been maltreated.

Despite those who raised the cry of sacrilege, or insisted that there were far better antidotes to Fenianism, Gladstone led Parliament in the disestablishment and partial disendowment of the Church of Ireland (the Anglican Church in Ireland). After 1869 the Irish Catholics could no longer complain that they had to contribute to the support of an alien church. Gladstone was also responsible for the passage of the Land Act of 1870, the purpose of which was to improve the position of the Irish tenant farmer and to facilitate land purchase. Though the measure was mild in its provisions and though it turned out to be largely unworkable, it was important in its implications. A Parliament dominated by Liberals abandoned the idea of self-help by intervening in behalf of Irish tenants and limiting the property rights of Irish landlords.

By the time Gladstone ended his first ministry in 1874, the depression had begun, and it became intense under the Conservative government that followed. But Disraeli had long since abandoned a view that he had expressed some thirty years before, that the duty of an English minister dealing with Irish problems was to "effect by his policy all those changes which a Revolution would do by force." If the Disraeli government did virtually nothing to lessen the impact of the depression on Ireland, it was because of the widespread expectation that the economic distress, still generally believed to be the product of unfortunate weather, would soon end. So it was that Ireland, a country with a dangerously lopsided economy that was almost entirely dependent on farming, felt the full weight of falling agricultural prices and increasing foreign competition. Tenants, unable to meet their obligations, were evicted, and landlords converted arable land to pasture. Instances of peasant violence against landlords, of which there was a long tradition in Ireland, multiplied.

The Land for the People.   In these circumstances, Michael Davitt, friend of Henry George, founded the Land League with its slogan, "The Land for the people." Davitt came from a peasant family which had been evicted when he was still a child. At the age of eleven he lost an arm in an accident at his job in Lancashire. In time he became a Fenian, but while in prison for his revolutionary activities he changed his mind about the Irish question: its answer was not so much political as economic. Davitt's League flourished because of the depression. Peasants flocked to it because they did not want to be depression casualties; they wanted protection against eviction and exorbitant rents. (*See Document No. 23.*)

Davitt formed an alliance with the Irish home rulers in Parliament. This group had been formed in 1870 by the Protestant Dublin lawyer, Isaac Butt, a moderate and thoughtful former professor of political economy who hoped by gentle persuasion to convince the English of the merits of the Irish case for autonomy in strictly domestic matters. One of the most important arguments that Butt and his followers used was that a parliament in Dublin would serve as a genuinely conservative element in the structure of British politics; it would protect Ireland against revolutionary tendencies. The Irish home rulers increased unexpectedly in the years after the secret ballot was adopted in 1872, for voters now felt free not to vote for the candidates preferred by their social superiors. There was, nevertheless, no widespread interest in home rule on the part of the bulk of the Irish peasantry. What gave the home rule movement importance was its alliance with the Land League; in other words, it was the agricultural depression that worked to interest the masses in

home rule. Political and land reform were now linked.
The home rulers would back land reform, and the land
reformers would support home rule. The Irish Protestant
landlord, Charles Stewart Parnell, who had displaced
Butt as effective leader of the home rulers, became president of the Land League, though he despised the social
radicalism of Davitt and his extremist friends. The Irish
nationalists in Parliament thus became a party with an
enormous following at home; and they were receiving
funds from Irish-Americans who delighted in the way
they were forcing attention to Irish problems by the use
of obstructionist tactics in Parliament. No one could
say of them that there was nothing and nobody behind
them.

Gladstone Tries. During his second ministry (1880-
1885), Gladstone took further steps to remove Irish grievances, insisting that in view of the distress of Irish peasants the ordinary rules of property could not be applied.
In 1881 he was responsible for the passage of a new Land
Act which granted to the tenants the famous three F's
(*fair rent, free sale, fixed tenure*). The significance of this
law can hardly be exaggerated, for the Liberal Party had
accepted a dual conception of property: tenants as well
as landlords had important rights in the land. The measure also made provision for the transformation of tenants
into peasant proprietors. Even so, unrest continued, for
some members of the Land League wanted land nationalization; they complained that the Land Act did not go far
enough. Gladstone's second ministry was, therefore, much
occupied with the discussion of coercion laws, which, by
suspending the normal liberties of the citizen, were designed to check violence and crime and restore order in
Ireland. Englishmen hated the coercion laws, but they
hated even more the disorders that made them necessary.
Indeed, the damage done to the Irish cause in English
minds by these disorders was immense. Samuel Butler,
completing *The Way of All Flesh* in the early 1880's, had
Theobald Pontifex ask, "What is this horrid government
going to do with Ireland?" And Tennyson's lines in
"Locksley Hall Sixty Years After" were filled with meaning for his contemporaries:

Have we grown at last beyond the passions of the
    primal clan?
'Kill your enemy, for you hate him,' still, 'your
    enemy' was a man.

Have we sunk below them? peasants maim the
    helpless horse, and drive
Innocent cattle under thatch, and burn the kindlier
    brutes alive.

Brutes, the brutes are not your wrongers—burnt at
    midnight, found at morn,
Twisted hard in mortal agony with their offspring,
    born-unborn,

Clinging to the silent mother! Are we devils? are
    we men?
Sweet Saint Francis of Assisi, would that he were
    here again . . .

A Parliament in Dublin.   With the extension of the
suffrage in 1884—the Irish electorate was trebled—and
with the redistribution of parliamentary seats in 1885,
Parnell's home rulers became even more powerful, so
much so, that rumors circulated that one of the leading
parties would endorse Irish self-government. Some of
Gladstone's closest colleagues knew that ever since the
seventies he had been moving in this direction, but he had
kept his conversion secret in the hope that it might be possible for the Irish and the Conservatives to reach an understanding about home rule. He could then bring the
Liberal Party around, and so it would be possible to keep
the discussion of Ireland's political future from degen-
erating into an ugly controversy. This hope was not realized, for, owing to the indiscretion of his son Herbert,
word leaked out in December, 1885 that Gladstone had
been converted to home rule for Ireland. (*See Document
No. 24.*)

In 1886 he introduced his home rule bill, and the attacks on him—"Old Billy Gladstone's a traitor"—were
many as well as venomous. He was widely denounced as
"a force for disturbance, the Alaric of his world, not the
man to conserve and consolidate a State but the man to
destroy it." Nor was this reaction a surprise, for, as J. L.
Hammond has pointed out in an important book on

Gladstone and the Irish Nation, the Liberal leader challenged two of the fixed ideas of his generation: the belief that the English social system suited Ireland and the belief that Ireland would retain its traditional political position in the United Kingdom. Gladstone split his party. Joseph Chamberlain and others became Liberal Unionists, whose main purpose was to preserve the Act of Union with Ireland and to prevent the establishment of a separate parliament in Dublin. After the most absorbing political debate that Thomas Hardy and millions of other late Victorians could remember, Liberal Unionists and Conservatives defeated the first home rule bill. Among many others, Matthew Arnold, friend of culture and enemy of anarchy, rejoiced; he had worried because Gladstone's middle-class Liberals were "so enthusiastically devoted to him, and so ignorant." (*See Document No. 25.*) Gladstone's eloquence—"Think, I beseech you, think well, think wisely, think, not for the moment, but for the years that are to come, before you reject this Bill"—had failed; and as Chamberlain walked by in the lobby of the House, Parnell could cry out that there went the man who killed home rule. The fact was, however, that even if the bill had passed the House of Commons it would have been rejected by the House of Lords.

Though Gladstone was not far from eighty at the time of the defeat of the first home rule bill, he did not give up the fight for a separate legislature for Ireland. In the next years he worked hard to educate the voters and to bring them around to his way of thinking. As G. M. Young has so admirably said: "Released from power, the old man employed the most wonderful resources of voice, presence, experience, fame, of scholarly and religious accomplishment, ever given to an English statesman, to keep Ireland before the eyes of a people already stirring away from Liberalism towards an Imperialism or a collectivism of which he understood nothing." Gladstone was obsessed with the Irish problem; his friends complained that they could get him to talk about nothing else—not even Homer. When, during his fourth and last ministry (1892-1894), he at last introduced a second home rule bill, it was thrown out by the House of Lords.

The Conservatives and Liberal Unionists, coming to

power in 1895, had no intention of satisfying Irish national aspirations. They resumed their attempt to kill
home rule with kindness—with material concessions. They
continued their policy of encouraging land purchase measures which they had begun in 1885 with the Ashbourne
Act—state-assisted land purchase laws which had the
effect of converting Ireland into a country of peasant proprietors. The Unionists also passed legislation to encourage the development of rural industries, coöperative societies, and fisheries. Home rule, however, was out of the
question; they would use strong government to keep it
down. But even the staunchest anti-home rulers did not
think the matter settled; nationalism was stronger than
ever in Ireland. Well could King Paramount the First in
Gilbert and Sullivan's *Utopia, Limited* (1893) sing:

> Great Britain is that monarchy sublime,
> To which some add (but others do not) Ireland.

Anti-Home Rulers.   Critics of home rule came from
every section of the English population—from the lowliest workers to the most eminent aristocrats; so Gladstone was not wholly accurate when he said to those who
fought his bill of 1886: "You have power, you have
wealth, you have rank, you have station, you have organisation." Regardless of their social background, however,
the opponents of home rule insisted that it meant the disintegration of the empire; it was the stepping-stone to
separation. Even though Gladstone's bills of 1886 and
1893 asserted the supremacy of the imperial Parliament
and granted only limited authority to the proposed separate parliament in Dublin, anti-home rulers remained un-
convinced. In part their opposition was based on military
considerations. Through the centuries, they argued, the
Irish had taken advantage of English difficulties: in
the sixteenth century they joined with Philip II against the
Elizabethans; in the seventeenth they fought on the side
of Louis XIV; in the eighteenth they sided with the
French revolutionaries. In view of this long tradition of
infamy, the Irish could not be trusted. Give them home
rule and they would threaten English military security all
the more.

The opposition to home rule was also partly religious.

Since home rule would mean *Rome* rule, the argument ran, how could Protestant Englishmen permit their co-religionists in Ireland to come under the rule of Roman Catholics who would swamp and oppress them? The appeal of Lord Randolph Churchill's slogan, "Ulster will fight, Ulster will be right," was strong. Sometimes the opposition to home rule was racist. The Irish, it was said, were temperamental, excitable, and inferior Celts who were utterly incompetent to rule themselves. Ability to govern was not in their blood; they had insufficient regard for life, order, and property. Could people who had recently engaged in so much arson, intimidation, murder, and violence in general be trusted with autonomy? Grant them a parliament and blood would run in the streets.

The hostility to home rule was also partly economic. If the Irish achieved self-government, they would soon, some people contended, impose tariff barriers, and the English, already damaged badly by the protectionism of their German, American, and French competitors, would suffer all the more. Had not Parnell insisted in a number of speeches that to foster the development of Irish industries the parliament in Dublin would favor protective tariffs against English goods?

Arguments of the Home Rulers. Supporters of home rule denied the validity of the military, religious, racist, economic, and other arguments advanced by the critics of home rule. What they emphasized above all was the growth of Irish nationalism, which they considered inextinguishable. The vast majority of the Irish people detested being governed by England; they were solidly behind the idea of self-government. Better, therefore, yield while the yielding could be done gracefully. In Gladstone's words: "The difference between giving with freedom and dignity on the one side, with acknowledgment and gratitude on the other, and giving under compulsion—giving with disgrace, giving with resentment dogging you at every step of your path—this difference is, in our eyes, fundamental. . . ." The whole tendency of the nineteenth century favored the growth of national self-consciousness. For the English to refuse to recognize Irish nationalism was for them to defy the course of history. Home rule, in a word, was the way to guarantee

English security; a self-governing Ireland would be content and, therefore, a source of strength to England. To quote Gladstone again: "Gentlemen speak of tightening the ties between England and Ireland as if tightening the tie were always the means to be adopted. Tightening the tie is frequently the means of making it burst, whilst relaxing the tie is very frequently the way to provide for its durability, and to enable it to stand a stronger strain. . . ."

Cromwell's Legacy. While the Irish did not gain home rule in the late Victorian era, they won a major series of concessions from the English: disestablishment, land acts which improved the position of tenants, and land purchase acts which were to change Ireland into a country of peasant proprietors. Furthermore, the decline in the size of the population reduced the pressure of people on limited Irish resources; and Sir Horace Plunkett's Irish Agricultural Organization Society did amazing work in encouraging a more scientific approach to farming. Even so, no one could have said that Anglo-Irish relations were amicable as the nineteenth century closed. The reason is not only that the Irish had failed to secure home rule. Above all, perhaps, the explanation is that what made the Irish people Irish was their hatred of the English; for them to stop hating England was for them to cease to be Irish. As the late Victorian period ended, Cromwell was more alive than he had been in the era of the Puritan Revolution: there was a much bigger and a much more bitter population to loathe him in an age when England, rather than the weather and the world economy, was blamed for the sufferings and losses of the Irish.

CLAMOR FOR EMPIRE

The New Imperialism. In the generation before the great depression the British Empire expanded territorially, but the environment of ideas was often hostile to this expansion. In the age of the great depression—the period of the "new imperialism"—the formal empire continued to grow as in the past. This was nothing new. The big difference came in the climate of opinion. While the old anti-imperialist sentiments certainly did not disappear, they diminished relatively in importance. Fervent advocates of empire became increasingly prominent, and not surprisingly they based their defense of expansion on the effects of the great depression. Economic distress played a decisive part in arousing and intensifying interest in empire. At a time when German and American competitors were threatening the English economic position, patriots of all classes came to look on imperialism and schemes of imperial federation as devices to avert the decline of their country.

Colonies Do Not Pay. It would be a mistake to ignore or to underestimate the rôle of critics of imperialism on the late Victorian scene, for in Parliament and the colonial office there were people in policy-making positions who continued to echo the beliefs of such outspoken anti-imperialists as Richard Cobden and Goldwin Smith. To cite two striking examples: Gladstone had been much influenced by the views of Cobden, and Cobden's friend and colleague of long standing, John Bright, sat in the House of Commons until late in the nineteenth century. It was not only that high-ranking members of the Liberal Party held anti-expansionist views; so, too, did large numbers of ordinary Liberal M.P.'s.

Critics of imperialism believed that colonies were an expense and a source of military weakness. As Goldwin Smith, Regius Professor of Modern History at Oxford,

put it in his letters to the *Daily News* that were reprinted
in book form as *The Empire* (1863): "To protect dependent Colonies we not only burden our overtaxed people with gratuitous taxation, but scatter our forces, naval
as well as military, over the globe, leaving the heart of
England open to a sudden blow. What do we gain in return?" His answer: "no advantage at all." Tennyson, who
rarely let an opportunity pass to use his poetry to express
his views on current affairs, described anti-imperialism,
which he opposed, in these lines that he added in 1872 to
The Idylls of the King:

> And that true North [Canada], whereof we lately
> heard
> A strain to shame us, 'Keep you to yourselves;
> So loyal is too costly! friends—your love
> Is but a burthen: loose the bond, and go.'
> Is this the tone of empire? here the faith
> That made us rulers?

Like Smith, critics of imperialism denied the validity of
the arguments set forth by those who wished to maintain
and extend the empire. They considered the amount of
colonial trade negligible; the United States was a far better customer than Canada. They dismissed the use of
colonies as outlets for surplus population; above all, emigrants were going to the United States. And they ridiculed
the defense of empire for reasons of glory, patriotism, and
prestige. Small wonder that they favored speeding up the
transformation of dependencies into independent nations.
While they never tired of comparing a colony with a
"child, who, grown to manhood, leaves his father's house
to win wealth and honours of his own," they often complained that the child either refused to grow up or having
grown up still remained too dependent on his father.
They found the lack of financial self-reliance especially
exasperating. As Sir Charles Dilke phrased it in his travel
book on *Greater Britain* (1868): "No reason presents itself . . . why our artisans and merchants should be taxed
in aid of populations far more wealthy than our own, who
have not, as we have, millions of paupers to support. We
at present tax our humblest classes, we weaken our defences, we scatter our troops and fleets, and lay ourselves

open to panics . . . in order to protect against imaginary dangers the Australian gold-digger and the Canadian farmer." But some of the most ardent foes of imperialism defended the retention of India. Goldwin Smith reasoned that the emancipation of India would bring chaos; it would mean "to do a great wrong to the people in addition to those which have already been done." Similarly, Dilke argued that if the English left India anarchy would follow.

In the debate over imperialism, Disraeli's Crystal Palace address of 1872 was of central importance. Reading reports of it in their newspapers, Englishmen could never have guessed that only a few years before Disraeli had written to Lord Derby: "Leave the Canadians to defend themselves; recall the African squadron; give up the settlements on the west coast of Africa; and we shall make a saving which will, at the same time, enable us to build ships and have a good Budget." In the same letter of 1866 he made it clear that he wanted the English to exercise power and influence in Asia, but that he had no use for "colonial deadweights," of which he considered Canada the prime example. Disraeli's position was strikingly close to that of Richard Cobden, who shortly before his death in 1865 was urging Canadian independence, and to that of John Bright, who also spoke up for an independent Canada which would maintain its own defences, fight for its own causes, and build its own future without depending on the English. Disraeli's conversion to a vigorous imperialism by 1872 was due to his awareness of the need for a program that would help to defeat Gladstone's Liberals and bring the Conservative Party to power. It was also due to his concern over the growth of republican and anti-monarchical agitation in the early seventies. Charles Bradlaugh, Dilke, and the members of some eighty republican clubs were urging that the crown be abolished. Disraeli believed that the cry of empire would arouse loyalty to the monarchy and defeat the republican agitators.

The Respect of the World. In his Crystal Palace speech Disraeli condemned the Liberals for their efforts "so continuous, so subtle, supported by so much energy, and carried on with so much ability and acumen" to bring about the disintegration of the empire. "It has been proved to all of us," he noted, "that we have lost money by our Colonies. It has been shown with precise, with mathematical demonstration, that there never was a jewel in the Crown of England that was so truly costly as the possession of India. How often has it been suggested that we should at once emancipate ourselves from this incubus!" Disraeli denounced the Liberals for having viewed the colonies simply from an economic point of view and for having totally ignored "those moral and political considerations which make nations great, and by the influence of which alone men are distinguished from animals." Rejoicing that the attempts of the Liberals to dismember the empire had failed, he made it plain that the duty of an English minister was to reconstruct and strengthen imperial relations. Not content with an England that was simply a comfortable land, he saw her as "a great country, an Imperial country, a country where your sons, when they rise, rise to paramount positions, and obtain not merely the esteem of their countrymen, but command the respect of the world." Like Tennyson, he did not want England to become a "third-rate isle half-lost among her seas."

Disraeli certainly made his countrymen empire-conscious during his ministry from 1874 to 1880, when, among other events of imperial significance, Fiji was annexed, the Suez Canal shares were purchased, the Queen was proclaimed Empress of India, Turkey was protected against Russian expansionism, Cyprus was acquired, and the Zulus were defeated. Even Gladstone, though he objected to the Conservatives' attempt to "cajole or drive us into Imperialism," was saying by 1878: "The sentiment of empire may be called innate in every Briton. If there are exceptions, they are like those of men born blind or lame among us. It is part of our patrimony: born with our birth, dying only with our death; incorporating itself in the first elements of our knowledge, and interwoven with all our habits of mental action upon public affairs."

By the time Disraeli's ministry ended, the great depression was well under way, and it continued in the eighties. No wonder publicists came to restate the case for imperialism in economic terms, attempting to convince Englishmen of all classes that the salvation of their country depended on the retention and expansion of their empire. In what quickly became a classic, *The Expansion of England* (1883), John Robert Seeley, professor of modern history at Cambridge, emphasized that colonies offered land for the landless and the prospect of wealth for those in financial distress; and since no nation in all history was "half so much cramped for want of room" as the England of his day, it was reassuring that this surplus population could move to colonies and continue to remain Britons. Seeley predicted that in another fifty years the United States and Russia would tower over countries like Germany and France. They would also dwarf England completely unless her people stopped thinking of themselves simply as a European power and started thinking of themselves as a vast but widely dispersed English nation.

Pressure from Other Nations.   Three years after the appearance of *The Expansion of England,* James Anthony Froude, the eminent historian of the Tudors and author of a sympathetic biography of Disraeli, brought out his *Oceana.* To justify his appeal for a commonwealth of Oceana that would be held together by common ancestry, interest, and pride, he stressed the decline of the English economic position: "Other nations press us with their rivalries. Expenses increase, manufactures languish or cease to profit." Froude granted that in time business would probably improve, but he argued that its further growth would be erratic. It was time, therefore, to take steps to bring the United Kingdom, Canada, South Africa, Australia, and New Zealand into a commonwealth of Oceana. "In the multiplying number of our own fellow-citizens animated by a common spirit," he said, "we should have purchasers for our goods from whom we should fear no rivalry; we should turn in upon them the tide of our emigrants which now flows away, while the emigrants themselves would thrive under their own fig tree, and rear children with stout limbs and colour in their cheeks, and a chance before them of a human existence." (*See Document No. 26.*)

Empire and Imaginative Literature.   The agitation for empire was not confined to non-fiction; it is significant that in the late Victorian period works of imaginative

literature increasingly dealt with the imperial theme.
Tennyson, Rudyard Kipling, W. E. Henley, and Alfred
Austin figured most prominently among the writers who
sought to arouse interest in British lands overseas. (*See
Document No. 28.*) Indeed, Kipling's public reputation
became so linked with imperialism—with what he called
in *Something of Myself* "the whole sweep and meaning of
things and effort and origins throughout the Empire"—
that his merits as a creative writer have often been be-
littled in the anti-imperialist atmosphere of recent times.
In the late nineteenth century, however, things were different. In an important book, *Novels of Empire*, Professor Susanne Howe Nobbe has stressed the popularity of
such works at that time: "They took the tired Victorian
out of mean streets, hospitals, prisons, into good English
fresh air again. (Even if it was tropical air it was chiefly
English-owned). They took him out of the long, level,
semidetached chronicles of drab lives and nether worlds,
to places where people could frankly take sides again and
sportsmanship was valued. . . . The writers about empire gave him as much good red-blooded adventure as
Stevenson, and left him with the comfortable feeling that
realism had not been sacrificed either."

Empire and Politics.   Politicians, too, in the age of
the great depression showed more interest in the possibilities of empire. Lord Rosebery, the Liberal leader, who
was to succeed Gladstone in 1894 as Prime Minister,
became an enthusiastic imperialist in the eighties. In
speeches to labor groups and organizations of businessmen, he tried to communicate to others that feeling for
empire which had become the dominant passion of his
public life. In an address to the Leeds Chamber of Commerce, for instance, he rejoiced that hostility to empire,
once so strong in England, had for the most part ceased,
and he went out of his way to remind his audience of the
value of colonial customers. On a per capita basis Canada
imported English goods worth nearly three and a half
times more than what the United States bought from
England. And Australia, with its tiny population, imported as much from England as the United States with
its almost sixty million people.

Lord Salisbury was also impressed with the economics

of empire. Salisbury, who had already served as Prime
Minister in the Conservative governments of 1885 and
1886-92, announced in the House of Lords shortly before
he began his third ministry in 1895 that it was the responsibility of the government to make things easy in new
imperial areas for commerce, enterprise, and capital—the
more so because protective tariffs were closing so many
of the traditional outlets for "the commercial energies of
our race." Lord Salisbury was blunt in insisting that the
government was duty-bound to use every opportunity to
open new regions for English trade. Uganda, for example,
a fertile and a heavily populated area, had tremendous
economic possibilities, and it was important that English
businessmen have free access to the country. Hence he
addressed to Lord Rosebery's Liberal Government these
strong words: "You must open the path. It is for you to
make the communication. It is for you to enable our people to get there. It is for you to enable capital to be invested and commerce to be extended."

Opening Up Markets. Above all, however, the late
Victorian politician who saw in imperialism the way out
of the depression was Joseph Chamberlain, the former
Liberal who had become a Liberal Unionist over the
home rule question. In 1895 Chamberlain became Secretary of State for the Colonies in Salisbury's third Conservative ministry, and he explained his acceptance of this
post in these words: "It is because I desire to see whether
there may not be room for still further developing our
resources in these new countries and for opening up British markets." Chamberlain was convinced of the importance of looking for remedies that would end bad trade
and unemployment. (*See Document No. 27.*) Although
the population continued to grow, commerce and industry were not developing proportionately. Germany, the
United States, and other countries were trying to stop
buying goods from Britain and at the same time they were
attempting to undersell the British in their own markets.
Because of foreign competition, hostile tariffs, and the use
by rivals of bounties and subsidies, the British need for
fresh markets was especially urgent; without new customers, bad trade and unemployment would become
chronic. Chamberlain's point was that, on the one hand,

Britain had to develop the resources of territories she already owned; on the other, she had to extend those possessions. No late Victorian could doubt that Chamberlain believed in the British Empire, for his efforts to maintain and to expand it were many. During his tenure of office, West Africa was reorganized, imperial road and railroad building were encouraged, the study of tropical medicine and agriculture was furthered, development loans were granted, and the Boer War was fought with generous support from Canada, Australia, and New Zealand. In time Chamberlain became convinced that to avert "the disasters which will infallibly come upon us" it was necessary to take steps to keep British trade in British hands. Even under the most promising conditions tariff reform was politically dangerous, for the bulk of the electorate, the working classes, viewed it as synonymous with higher food prices. But Chamberlain's conversion to tariff reform came not under the most promising conditions but at an impossible time, for towards the turn of the century the depression ended, and prices and profits started to climb. It is not strange, therefore, that his demand for tariff reform split the Conservative Party and helped prepare the way for the triumph of the Liberals in 1906.

The extension of the Empire in late Victorian times reflected the growth of imperialist sentiments among voters; and the growth of these sentiments was inseparable from the fears generated by the depression. But if the Empire was not extended even more than it was in the last decades of the nineteenth century, one main explanation is that there remained a strong element in the population that either doubted or denied the arguments of the imperialists. These people still insisted that colonies were not worthwhile. It was bad enough that they were a financial burden; worse still, they were a military risk. To support their position, critics pointed to the string of war scares involving Russia, Germany, the United States, and France that took place in the late Victorian period; and *The War of the Worlds* (1898) by H. G. Wells, then a young writer of science-fiction, suggested the horrors of warfare in an age of advanced technology. Critics were agitated by the German Emperor's announcement in 1896 that Germany's future lay on the water and by the

passage two years later of the German Navy Law, and
they demonstrated how articulate they were during the
Boer War (1899-1902). They felt strongly about the
main issue over which the war was fought—whether
the British or the Boers should dominate South Africa.
They detested Cecil Rhodes and denounced his plan to
make all of South Africa British and to join it to the
North by a Cape to Cairo railway. Even as Victoria died
they were saying that Britain should not have been in
South Africa in the first place. Surrounded by European
enemies, she had to conserve her resources.

— 10 —

CONCLUSION

An Age of Tension. The great depression of 1873-
1896 provides an invaluable key to an understanding of
late Victorian history: to the ruin of agriculture, the decline of commercial and industrial leadership, the improvement of the condition of the working classes, the
growth of faith in technical education, the development
of state intervention in social and economic affairs, the
proliferation of social action groups in the churches, the
spread of socialism, the deterioration of Anglo-Irish relations, and the intensification of interest in imperialism.
If the late Victorians found much to disturb them, it was
no surprise. They had so many difficult problems to solve
—or at least to live with—that it would have seemed incredible to them that a later generation would find theirs
a golden and a self-complacent age. They would have
insisted rather that they lived in an era of tension when

little was right with the world. They could find consolation in the fact that so many of the difficulties with which they had to contend plagued not only England but in varying degrees all the major powers in the last decades of the nineteenth century. By and large, however, they would have agreed with Matthew Arnold when in the midst of the home rule controversy he wrote to a friend: "I suppose things looked even worse for us at the end of the last century, but to my eye they look extremely bad now." And they knew what Tennyson meant when in "Locksley Hall Sixty Years After" (1886) he asked, "When was age so cramm'd with menace? madness? written, spoken lies?" It is not fortuitous that so many a late Victorian autobiographer expressed the hope that "in troublous times like ours" the story of his life might console and reassure his contemporaries.

Strachey's Offensive against the Victorians. No modern writer has shaped current attitudes towards Victorian England so much as Lytton Strachey. This fact makes many historians writhe, for they take a dim view of Strachey and his *Eminent Victorians*. They dislike his frivolity, his condescension, his iconoclasm, his inadequate research, and his unwillingness to view the Victorians in the light of their times; and they refuse to recognize that in many respects Strachey himself was a late Victorian who engaged in the increasingly favorite late Victorian enterprise of revolting against parents. Patriotic English historians, in particular, have never been able to forgive him. They cannot forget that he published his attacks on the Victorians in the last year of World War I. At a time when the future of England looked so bleak, there was Strachey attacking the English past.

Historians grant that Strachey knew how to write, but they have great misgivings about the misinterpretations he has spread and the myths he has fostered. Small wonder, therefore, that whenever the opportunity presents itself they caution readers to avoid Strachey or at least not to take him seriously—to view his *Eminent Victorians* as a piece of imaginative literature. And they urge readers to turn to such outstanding historians as Elie Halévy, R. C. K. Ensor, and G. M. Young, all of whom have written profoundly about the problems of the Victorians.

For all their efforts, anti-Stracheyite historians have failed notoriously, for *Eminent Victorians* gives every sign of enduring for a long time. Now, more than a generation since its publication, it is clear that it can be replaced only by a work written by a scholar who has the knowledge and understanding of an Halévy, an Ensor, and a Young and the literary gifts of a Strachey. Unfortunately, such a historian appears only rarely—almost as rarely as a Gladstone or a Ruskin. Doubtless, therefore, Strachey will march on as the chief shaper of twentieth-century views of the Victorians.

Part II

DOCUMENTS
FROM THE LATE VICTORIAN
PERIOD

— Reading No. 1 —

THE ROYAL COMMISSION REPORTS ON THE CAUSES OF AGRICULTURAL DEPRESSION, 1882[1]

Rural distress became so intense and widespread by the late 1870's that Disraeli's government yielded to demands for the appointment of a Royal Commission to investigate the causes of the depression and to suggest remedies. The Commission accumulated a vast amount of evidence which reveals what landowners, farmers, and agricultural laborers thought about their plight. The Commission itself singled out foreign competition as a main cause of the depression, but it stressed above all the rôle of bad weather—an indication of the slowness of contemporaries to recognize the changes that were taking place in the world economy.

✓   ✓   ✓

Of the immediate causes of agricultural depression it cannot be said that any one of them is necessarily of a "permanent character." Bad and good seasons appear to come in cycles, and with them alternations of agricultural prosperity or depression.

This, the main cause of depression, no legislation can control.

How far foreign competition may affect the home producer in the future it is impossible to calculate with any

[1] "Report from Her Majesty's Commissioners on Agriculture," *Parliamentary Papers*, 1882, XIV, 32-33.

degree of certainty. That its effect will continue to be felt may be assumed as certain.

It is to be hoped that the proposals which we have made will, if adopted, eventually place all classes connected with land in a better position to meet those difficulties to which they are necessarily exposed, and which are sure to be, as they always have been, of periodical recurrence.

We have already indicated various matters upon which legislative interference can benefit directly the agricultural classes of this country. But no interference between classes, between owners and occupiers, or between employers and labourers, can render any one of them independent of the other. We cannot recall a period in our history in which the relations of these classes have been more severely tried than during the existing depression. Owners have, as a rule, borne their share of a common calamity, and they, as well as occupiers, have done much to avert the distress from the class who are least able to bear it. It is satisfactory to know that, as we have already observed, upon the labourer it has fallen more lightly than upon either owner or occupier. The best hope for the prosperity of agriculture lies in the mutual confidence and friendly relations of the three classes directly engaged in it, and in the common conviction that their interests are inseparable.

In concluding this Report we may be allowed to record our opinion that the condition of British agriculture has never been the subject of a more comprehensive and laborious inquiry than that in which we have been engaged. The mass of evidence which we have now the honour to submit for Your Majesty's consideration, collected, we believe, with the greatest care and impartiality, presents an exhaustive record of the extent and immediate effects of the agricultural depression, of the causes to which that depression may be attributed, and of the various suggestions submitted to us from opposite points of view for ameliorating the condition of the agricultural classes.

ANOTHER ROYAL COMMISSION DISCUSSES THE CAUSES OF AGRICULTURAL DEPRESSION, 1897 [2]

Although the weather improved, rural distress continued. Again a Royal Commission was appointed, and, when it issued its final report in 1897, it went into great detail concerning the growth of world agricultural production. It pointed out that farmers in other countries had many advantages that the English lacked; above all, they could raise their products much more cheaply. Therefore, as long as England continued its free trade policies, the rural community would have to adapt itself to the realities of foreign competition.

✓   ✓   ✓

. . . It is clear that there has been a remarkable increase in the imports of all forms of agricultural produce during the past 20 years.

Of the various products of British agriculture, wheat has been the most affected by this development, the foreign supply of this grain having gradually displaced the home production until the latter now constitutes barely 25 per cent. of the total quantity needed for consumption annually in this country. There has been no similar displacement of the other home-grown cereals, but in the case of barley it is worthy of notice that the low-priced varieties grown in Eastern Europe, which were imported in comparatively small quantities in 1876-80, now form the larger proportion of the foreign supply, and this

[2] "Final Report of Her Majesty's Commissioners Appointed to Inquire into the Subject of Agricultural Depression," *Parliamentary Papers*, 1897, XV, 85-87.

change has been of some influence in the determination
of the price of British barley. . . .

As regards meat we have been unable to trace any ac-
tual displacement of the home produce by the growth of
the imports. The supply of foreign beef and mutton apparently meets a demand for cheap meat which has not
hitherto been satisfied by the home production, and while
it has undoubtedly seriously affected the price of the inferior grades of British produce, its influence on the superior qualities has been much less marked. Foreign competition has been, on the whole, perhaps more severe in
pork than in other classes of meat, but it has been confined mainly to bacon and hams.

In the case of wool, the facts at our disposal show that
there has been a progressive increase in the foreign supplies of this staple, and there has been some displacement
of the home-grown product. The net imports form so
large a proportion of the total supply that they must be an
important factor in the determination of the price of British wool.

With respect to the extent of the foreign competition in
dairy produce we have estimated that the importation of
butter, margarine, and cheese represents more than 50 per
cent. of the total quantities of these articles available annually for consumption. . . .

It is, we think, important to note that in nearly every
case . . . the expansion of the imports has been accompanied by a contraction in the price of the several products concerned, and that there has been a general corre-
spondence between the fall of price and intensity of
foreign competition.

An investigation as to the sources contributing to the
increasing volume of imports of agricultural produce has
shown that the United States has held the premier position
throughout the last 20 years in the supply of wheat and
meat, excluding mutton, while she has also contributed
the major portion of the imports of maize, although her
shipments in this article since 1890 have been exceeded
by those of Roumania. Argentina has in recent years
ranked next to the United States as an exporter of wheat
and meat to this country. Other prominent contributors

to the imports of cereals are Russia for wheat and barley and India for wheat alone, though the Indian supply has fallen off considerably. Australasia is responsible for the major portion of the imports of wool and mutton, and we have recently received large consignments of butter from this source. Denmark furnishes between 40 and 50 per cent. of the butter imported annually; Canada and the United States practically monopolise the import trade in cheese; while Holland supplies nearly the whole of the margarine. . . .

No detailed evidence has been placed before us as to how far the improvements in the means of transport have enabled producers abroad to maintain their consignments to British markets during a period of falling prices, but the witnesses who have referred to this subject have agreed that the development and improvement of the lines of communication by land and sea and the reduction of freight rates have facilitated the cultivation of the fertile areas in North and South America and in the Colonies, and have generally contributed in no small degree to the growth of foreign competition. . . .

We have now summarised the principal deductions to be drawn from the information at our disposal. While we have fully recognised the importance of the question as to how long foreign competition is likely to continue in its present intensity, the evidence we have received does not enable us to express any definite view on the point. There seems to be some ground for the opinion that the existing conditions are not such as to encourage the United States to continue to export wheat and meat to this country on the scale to which we have hitherto been accustomed, but so far as we can judge it would be a mistake to assume that that country has yet reached the limit of her productive and exporting capabilities, for it is generally agreed that with an improvement in prices the United States could maintain their present position as a competitor in British markets, though this must eventually become more and more difficult with the increasing demands of their population and with the diminishing area of the virgin soils in the west.

But although there may be visible limits to the competition of the United States, the agriculturists of Great Britain have now to reckon with a new competitor in South America. . . .

In Australia, too, we understand that there are great tracts of unbroken fertile land suitable for the production of wheat. . . .

Contrasting the natural and economic conditions existing in the several countries mentioned above and in Great Britain, we fear that there is no near prospect of any permanent abatement in the pressure of foreign competition.

— Reading No. 3 —

A TRADE UNION SONG OF AGRICULTURAL WORKERS [3]

Trade unionism had begun to spread among farm hands even before the beginning of the agricultural depression. As the depression became intense, trade union leaders were all the more determined to organize rural labor. In an atmosphere of falling agricultural prices, however, farmers had to keep their production costs low, and so they resisted the unionists. The song that follows by Howard Evans is typical of many that were written in the 1870's to lift the morale of unionists and would-be unionists. Since workers were often illiterate, songs served as an invaluable means of communication.

[3] Frederick Clifford, *The Agricultural Lock-Out of 1874* (Edinburgh, 1875), pp. 364-65.

OH DEAR! WHAT'LL BECOME OF US?

Tune—"Oh Dear! What Can the Matter Be?"

What's a labourer's prospect in this land of freedom?
Six young uns to keep, and twelve shillings to feed 'em,
A jail and a workhouse, for all those who need 'em:
  Pray what does a labourer lack?

> *Chorus*—Oh dear! what'll become of us?
>   Oh dear! what'll become of us?
>   Oh dear! what'll become of us?
>   If he should give us the sack.

Twelve shillings a-week, it'll just fill one belly;
But Bill, Tom, and Hal, Polly, Susan, and Nelly,
They eat all day long, my old woman'll tell ye;
  I only can just get a snack.
              Oh dear! etc.

There came an old chap, whom the Union engages,
To show the poor man how to go for more wages;
Says he, "Ask for more, and if Farmer Grumps rages,
  The Union will stand at your back."
              Oh dear! etc.

Says Grumps, "If you join, it will end in disaster;
How dare you offend such an excellent master?"
Says I, "If you say so, we'll join all the faster."
  Oh! he looked awfully black!
              Oh dear! etc.

He says, "In the harvest we're putting him quite about;"
Yet, if he'd be just, there'd be nothing to fight about;
But he swears he'll send us all to the right about,
  When he begins to get slack.
              Oh dear! etc.

There's plenty of work to be had by the willing,
With wages at double the paltry twelve shilling,
And land o'er the sea, to be had for the tilling,
  If he should tell us to pack.
              Oh dear! etc.

— Reading No. 4 —

JOSEPH ARCH ON HIS UNION OF FARM WORKERS 1882[4]

As the best-known agricultural trade union leader in England, Joseph Arch was summoned to appear before the Royal Commission on Agriculture. He had an opportunity as a witness to discuss his conception of trade unionism as a weapon to improve the standard of living of agricultural workers.

Is your union in any way a life assurance society?—They insure for sickness, and old age, and death.

Is it a burial club?—Yes, we allow 5£ for burial.

Is it a savings bank?—No.

Then to what extent are its funds strike funds?—To any extent, according as the members dispose of them.

Do you approve of strikes?—No, certainly not.

Have you ever calculated the gain or loss resulting from a strike?—No. Strikes are sometimes a necessity, but I say they are necessary evils. I do not like them, and I think they might be avoided; and this is where the farmers would never meet us. We have tried our utmost to get a board of arbitration, and they will not meet us fairly; because I maintain that the labourer has a right to send whomsoever he thinks well as a representative upon that board.

Do you think that there is not that good feeling between the farmers and the labourers that there used to be? —Do not talk about the good feeling; it is mockery to the agricultural labourer to talk about it so much; because the farmer has got all he could out of the labourer, and of

[4] "Minutes of Evidence Taken Before Her Majesty's Commissioners on Agriculture," *Parliamentary Papers,* 1882, XIV, 91, 93.

course it has been the labourer's duty to do the best he could. I only wish there was more of it. I never saw the good feeling, so I cannot give any idea of it. I believe that the relations of the labourers and the farmers are the same as they were when I was a boy.

You are speaking of yourself individually, from your own personal experience, rather than the opinion of the labourers themselves?—I think the labourers are all of that opinion more or less. . . .

Under what circumstances as to wages, rent, &c. do you consider that a labourer's condition would be such as to give him and you no just cause of complaint?—I would not answer that question.

It is not an improper one I hope?—I do not go on such paternal lines. I teach the labourer never to be satisfied while there is a chance of advancing in life. To teach a man to be content is to teach a man to curse himself; that is to say, you should increase within his mind a just discontent for every year of his life to make himself a better man, and his family more intelligent, and better fed, and better clothed.

Do you wish to convey to the Commission that your object in life, therefore, is to create agitation?—My object in life is to advise the labourer so long as he is in life not to rest satisfied with the results of 1881, but if he can do better in 1882 to do it, and if he can do better in 1883 to do it.

And you thereby teach him that he must never be satisfied?—I teach him that he must never be satisfied so long as there is a better prospect before him, and he thinks he has intelligence and brain and perseverance to reach after it.

— Reading No. 5 —

AGRICULTURAL WORKERS AND THE DEPRESSION, 1882[5]

The Royal Commission on Agriculture stated in 1882 that agricultural workers had suffered less from the depression than farmers or landowners. But trade union leaders insisted that this was an inaccurate conclusion, for workers had none of the resources on which to draw that farmers and landowners had available. When Alfred Simmons, for example, appeared as a witness before the Commission, he stressed the hardships of farm workers in an age of agricultural depression.

Mr. Alfred Simmons called in and examined.

You are, I believe, secretary of the Kent and Sussex Labourers' Union?—I am.

Can you tell the Commission with what object the Union was formed?—The Kent and Sussex Labourers' Union, I would like to say, is not associated with any other labourers' unions in the kingdom. Its objects were somewhat different from those of the labourers' union in the Midland counties, and for that reason it never has been associated with the Midland Counties Union. The objects were to secure increased wages for the agricultural labourer, to assist him with legal protection where necessary, (in county courts more particularly,) to assist him in emigration and migration, and to give him a general protection. . . .

With reference to the agricultural depression which we have recently experienced in this country, do you consider that the landlord, the tenant farmer, or the farm labourer

[5] "Minutes of Evidence Taken Before Her Majesty's Commissioners on Agriculture," *Parliamentary Papers,* 1882, XIV, 36, 47.

has suffered least?—I should say that the landlord suffers least. I should say that the farmer suffers most, but that he feels his suffering less than the labourer. To the labourer it is a question really of less food; to the farmer it is not absolutely a question of bread; it is comforts or no comforts. . . .

Then you consider that the labourer has suffered during the recent depression?—Most decidedly, I do.

— Reading No. 6 —

THE ROYAL COMMISSION ANALYZES THE COMMERCIAL AND INDUSTRIAL DEPRESSION, 1886[6]

If members of the rural community were loud in their complaints of hard times, merchants, manufacturers, and urban workers were hardly less loud. To look into their grievances a Royal Commission on Trade and Industry was appointed. Its final report, issued in 1886, analyzed the nature of the depression and recommended ways to meet the menace of foreign competition. The Commission was especially impressed with the need to extend and improve technical education.

[6] "Final Report of the Royal Commission Appointed to Inquire into the Depression of Trade and Industry; with Minutes of Evidence and Appendices," *Parliamentary Papers,* 1886, XXIII, x, xxiv.

Summarising very briefly the answers which we received to our questions, and the oral evidence given before us, there would appear to be a general agreement among those whom we consulted—

(*a*) that the trade and industry of the country are in a condition which may be fairly described as depressed;

(*b*) that by this depression is meant a diminution, and in some cases, an absence of profit, with a corresponding diminution of employment for the labouring classes;

(*c*) that neither the volume of trade nor the amount of capital invested therein has materially fallen off, though the latter has in many cases depreciated in value;

(*d*) that the depression above referred to dates from about the year 1875, and that, with the exception of a short period of prosperity enjoyed by certain branches of trade in the years 1880 to 1883, it has proceeded with tolerable uniformity and has affected the trade and industry of the country generally, but more especially those branches which are connected with agriculture. . . .

The great object to be aimed at is, we need hardly say, the cheapening of the cost of production so far as it can be done consistently with the maintenance of sound quality and good workmanship. In the competition for business, which has become so intense during the last few years, this will be the only means of securing success; and we have natural advantages in this respect such as are possessed by few of our rivals.

We think also that the increasing severity of the competition of foreign countries is a matter deserving more serious attention than it has received at the hands of our commercial and industrial classes. We cannot, perhaps, hope to maintain, to the same extent as heretofore, the lead which we formerly held among the manufacturing nations of the world. Various causes contributed to give us a position far in advance of other countries, which we were well able to hold for many years; but those causes could not have been expected to operate permanently, and our supremacy is now being assailed on all sides.

But if we do not possess to their full extent the same natural advantages as we formerly enjoyed, we have still the same physical and intellectual qualities which gave us so commanding a lead; and we see no reason why, with care, intelligence, enterprise, and thoroughness, we should not be able to continue to advance.

In order to do so, however, it is obvious that we must display greater activity in the search for new markets, and greater readiness to accommodate our productions to local tastes and peculiarities.

Even in matters of so little apparent importance as weights and measures it would seem that our disinclination to adapt ourselves to the requirements of our customers has not been without its effect.

In the matter of education we seem to be particularly deficient as compared with some of our foreign competitors; and this remark applies not only to what is usually called technical education, but to the ordinary commercial education which is required in mercantile houses, and especially the knowledge of foreign languages.

Suggestions have been offered by several witnesses as to the assistance which might be afforded to our trade by Your Majesty's Diplomatic and Consular Officers abroad, especially in reporting information with regard to the requirements of foreign markets, and in answering inquiries from merchants and others on such matters.

We gladly recognise the efforts which have been recently made to utilise the services of these officers more effectually; but we doubt if their functions could be usefully extended in the direction referred to above. It is very important, having regard to their position and duties in foreign countries, that they should be neither directly nor indirectly engaged in commercial operations, and we fear that inconvenience would be felt if they assumed in any degree the character of agents for mercantile houses.

Any general information which they may acquire with regard to the trade of the district in which they reside, and which is likely to be generally useful at home, should, of course, be reported and made public at once; and this is already provided for in their annual reports. But we should deprecate any change in their position which would bring them into closer relations with individual firms.

Nor do we think that it would be desirable for them to take a more active part in pressing particular schemes or enterprises set on foot by British traders in foreign countries. The representatives of some of our competitors may have been more active in this respect in some cases than our own consular and diplomatic officers; but such action must, we think, tend to lower the reputation of the country and to diminish the usefulness of the officer concerned.

— Reading No. 7 —

JOSEPH ARCH ON FREE TRADE AND PROTECTION, 1884[7]

Hard hit farmers and businessmen in the age of the great depression began to discuss seriously the possibility of abandoning England's free trade policy. This, they insisted, was the only way to meet foreign competition and end falling prices and profits. They called the form of protection they favored fair trade, and for a time in the 1880's it seemed that they were winning the support of influential leaders of the Conservative Party. The opposi-

[7] Joseph Arch, *Free Trade Versus Protection or Fair Trade, Weighed in the Balances and Found Wanting. Lessons from English History for English Working Men* (Coventry and London, 1884), Preface, ch. X.

tion to fair trade was especially pronounced among both rural and urban workers who feared that any departure from free trade would mean higher living costs. Joseph Arch's position was typical of that of the working classes.

✓   ✓   ✓

If the proposal to establish Fair Trade in this Country affected the Upper and Middle Classes solely, I do not think I should interest myself very much in the matter; not that I am indifferent to the welfare of either, but their means of information are so numerous and trustworthy, and their power to withstand adversity so superior to that of the working classes, that they may be very well left to form their own judgment, and look after themselves. With my brethren, the great wage-earning class, however, the aspect of the whole question is entirely changed. They have neither the time nor the opportunity for mastering the subject in all its variety of detail. To them much that is said and written by Statisticians and political economists, is senseless jargon. "Differential duties," "*Ad-valorem* duties," "Countervailing duties," and "Revenue duties," are Fair Trade phrases which fall upon the ear, only to perplex the mind; probably they are not always comprehended fully by those who use them so freely.

There is, however, a practical aspect of the question in regard to which the way-faring man, though a fool, will not err. He can understand facts where he stumbles at figures. When, therefore, the working man learns that the Protection Quartern Loaf, forty years ago, was 10d. and 1s., and remembers that the Free Trade Quartern Loaf is 5d. and 5½d., whatever else he fails to comprehend, that is a difference he can clearly understand. So can his wife and family. It is this practical aspect of the Fair Trade question—this plain matter-of-fact, bread-and-cheese view of it, with which I propose to deal in the following pages. The more intricate and speculative branches have been satisfactorily dealt with by others more gifted than myself. Mine are only plain words and undeniable facts, addressed with a feeling of confidence and sincerity to the common sense of the working men of England.

The following pages have been compiled in such odd moments as I found, from time to time, at my disposal.

To those who object to the fragmentary character of the work I must offer this as my excuse. I have quoted freely from the writings, reports, and evidence of others, because in the mouths of many witnesses a cause is established. But whatever the faults or merits of this book, if I succeed in awaking in the breasts of the working classes of England a sense of the perils to which they and their families are exposed by the attempt to re-establish "Protection" in this country, under the disguise of "Fair Trade," my object will be accomplished. . . .

A few concluding remarks and I will lay down my pen. I have shown you that Protection had a fair trial from 1815 to 1846, and that it signally failed. It plunged England into almost hopeless misery; it ruined trade; crippled commerce; it filled our gaols and workhouses, and it shortened the duration of human life; it drove trade from our shores; it made desolate the great centres of industry, and it smote, as with the hand of a deadly pestilence, the homes of the English working men. Riots and bloodshed were everywhere, the outward and visible signs of this cankerworm of protection, which was eating away the vitals of the country. I have further proved to you that Fair Trade is nothing more than a revival of that huge and wicked imposture. The old specious phrases and cant patriotism of Protection form the stock-in-trade of the Fair Trader. For evidence of the value of Free Trade, I fearlessly appeal to your own experience. You have had your own peculiar trials and sufferings, but you have never, not even in your darkest hours, experienced a tenth part of the hunger and starvation which the atrocious Corn Laws inflicted upon your forefathers. In your time, and in mine, there have been seasons of depression in trade, and particular industries have sometimes been brought almost to a standstill, but on no occasion has the general body of trade been so thoroughly and utterly paralyzed as it was in 1842, when the Corn Laws had their full fling and full play. You may occasionally have had short work, but you have never lacked a cheap loaf.

Now, with these facts before you, I ask, are you prepared to go back again into the House of Bondage? Are you willing, for the sake of keeping up the rents of the

Landlords, to pay again 1s. for your quartern loaf? Do
you wish to suffer the pangs of hunger, and the torments of
slow starvation; to see vessels laden with precious grain
emptied into the Thames, while your own children are
crying for bread? I ask these questions fearlessly, because
I have an unshaken confidence in the sound sense of the
working classes. I have unbounded faith in the perception
and courage of the working man. Theorists may endeav-
our to warp his judgment, and interested politicians may
strive to hoodwink his intelligence, but I have no misgiv-
ing as to the result. If the day should ever arrive when the
sons of toil in England are called upon to deliver their
verdict upon the question of Free Trade, I anticipate a
decision which shall for ever destroy the smallest chance
of resurrection of that greatest of all curses—the Corn
Laws!

— Reading No. 8 —

E. E. WILLIAMS' "MADE IN GERMANY," 1896 [8]

The concern to which growing foreign competition
gave rise in the late Victorian period was nowhere better
reflected than in E. E. Williams' *"Made in Germany."*
The volume had a phenomenal success because it dealt
with a topic that was on the minds of many Englishmen
and it appeared at a propitious time, for its publication

⁸ Ernest Edwin Williams, *"Made in Germany"* (London,
1896), pp. 10-11.

coincided with a deterioration in Anglo-German diplomatic relations.

1   *1*   *1*

"Made in Germany"

The phrase is fluent in the mouth: how universally appropriate it is, probably no one who has not made a special study of the matter is aware. Take observations, Gentle Reader, in your own surroundings: the mental exercise is recommended as an antidote to that form of self-sufficiency which our candid friends regard as indigenous to the British climate. Your investigations will work out somewhat in this fashion. You will find that the material of some of your own clothes was probably woven in Germany. Still more probable is it that some of your wife's garments are German importations; while it is practically beyond a doubt that the magnificent mantles and jackets wherein her maids array themselves on their Sundays out are German-made and German-sold, for only so could they be done at the figure. Your governess's *fiancé* is a clerk in the City; but he also was made in Germany. The toys, and the dolls, and the fairy books which your children maltreat in the nursery are made in Germany: nay, the material of your favourite (patriotic) newspaper had the same birthplace as like as not. Roam the house over, and the fateful mark will greet you at every turn, from the piano in your drawing-room to the mug on your kitchen dresser, blazoned though it be with the legend, *A Present from Margate*. Descend to your domestic depths, and you shall find your very drainpipes German made. You pick out of the grate the paper wrappings from a book consignment, and they also are "Made in Germany." You stuff them into the fire, and reflect that the poker in your hand was forged in Germany. As you rise from your hearthrug you knock over an ornament on your mantelpiece; picking up the pieces you read, on the bit that formed the base, "Manufactured in Germany." And you jot your dismal reflections down with a pencil that was made in Germany. At midnight your wife comes home from an opera which was made in Germany, has been here enacted by singers and conductor and players made in Germany, with the aid of instruments and sheets of music made in Germany. You go to bed, and glare wrathfully at a text on the wall; it is illuminated with an English village church, and it was "Printed in Germany." If you are imaginative and dyspeptic, you drop off to sleep only to dream that St. Peter (with a duly stamped halo round his head and a bunch of keys from the Rhineland) has refused you admission into Paradise, because you bear not the Mark of the Beast upon your forehead, and are not of German make. But you console yourself with the thought that it was only a Bierhaus Paradise anyway; and you are awakened in the morning by the sonorous brass of a German band.

— Reading No. 9 —

THE ADVANTAGES OF
ENGLAND'S RIVALS, 1897[9]

Several serious attempts were made in the late Victorian period to find out why foreign rivals were ousting English goods from market after market. In 1897 Joseph Chamberlain, then Colonial Secretary, made public a document that explained why even in the colonies particular English products were being displaced by those of rivals.

[9] Adapted from "Trade of the British Empire and Foreign Competition. Despatch from Mr. Chamberlain to the Governors of Colonies and the High Commissioner of Cyprus and the Replies Thereto," *Parliamentary Papers*, 1897, LX, 5-6.

Commodity	Nature of Displacement
APPAREL and slops of various kinds	Cheaper and more serviceable article. Low lines of goods well done.
ARMS and AMMUNITION: Firearms Gunpowder	Competition of a cheap and showy article.
BEER and ALE	The production of a lighter and more suitable drink.
CANDLES	Decidedly cheaper goods.
CEMENT	A finer grain, good quality, and lower price.
CHEMICAL PRODUCTS	Better manufacture, apparently depending on more skilled knowledge.
CLOCKS and WATCHES	Cheaper make, more attractive, more artistic, better-looking.
COTTON MANU-FACTURES	Cheaper goods of more showy character; special lines; especially in Stockings and Hosiery.
	Better cashmere.
	Inferior hosiery.
	Stockings better suited to market.
FURNITURE	Lighter and cheaper goods, quicker made.
GLASSWARE Lamp Chimneys	Better and cheaper goods. " " " "
HARDWARE	The States have a better name. There is more trouble taken to give variety. Cheaper goods, better suited.
Cutlery	Cheaper goods.
IMPLEMENTS and TOOLS of INDUS-TRY	Cheaper tool with lower freight. New patterns, more suitability.
	Effect of patents and advertising.

METALS:	
Iron and Steel	Cheaper price, and equally good or even better quality.
Nails	Cheaper price, and equally good or even better quality.
Wire Nails	Cheaper price, and equally good or even better quality.
Wire	Cheaper price, and equally good or even better quality.
Yellow Metal	Cheaper price, and equally good or even better quality.
PLATE and PLATED WARE	Novelty of design.
WOOLLEN MANU- FACTURES	Better designs in the finer goods. [Not much competition in heavier goods.]

— Reading No. 10 —

PROFESSOR LEVI ON THE CONDITION OF THE WORKING CLASSES, 1885 [10]

The condition of the working classes was the subject of several governmental and private investigations in the age of the great depression. The conclusions of these inquiries varied, but on one thing all investigators agreed: that the falling prices of the great depression were a great advantage to workers. One of the most sympathetic and

[10] Leone Levi, *Wages and Earnings of the Working Classes. Report to Sir Arthur Bass, M.P.* (London, 1885), pp. 38-40.

optimistic students of working-class conditions was Professor Levi, whose writings were frequently cited in late Victorian discussions of labor problems.

✓   ✓   ✓

Prospects of the Working Classes

It is time, however, for me to draw these observations to a close. Taken as a whole, the working classes of the United Kingdom may be said to be stronger in physique, better educated, with more time at their command, in the enjoyment of greater political rights, in a more healthful relation towards their employers, receiving higher wages, and better able to effect some savings in 1884, than they were in 1857; and if they are not satisfied with remaining at home on these conditions, their field of labour is wider than ever, emigration agents making the most tempting offers for their transport to the land of promise. I am not given to indulge in fancies or poetry. I prefer, with Swift,

> Leaving the wits the spacious air,
> With license to build castles there.

And I must remember that, "if the young dreamer glowering in the fire, laughing at the gusty flame, builds castles in the air, older eyes than his are dazzled by a glare, hearts are broken, and heads are turned with castles in the air." There is not much danger, however, in predicting that the future of the working classes is likely to be brighter than the past. It is something to say, that the era of servitude and ignorance, and the era of monopoly and privilege are past and for ever. But it is satisfactory to think that educated labour is likely to be in greater and greater request. Desponding minds see in any temporary diminution of trade and manufacture a sign of decadence and eventual relapse of British industry. I have no such fear. The world was never so open as it is now, despite the exclusive tariffs which improvident Governments have enacted, and the thousand millions and more of persons inhabiting it have scarcely realised the wealth that lies under their feet, and the vast benefits arising from intercommunion and commerce. The *rôle* of England may not be to provide France, or Italy, Germany or the United States, with merchandise which they can produce better for themselves. But by keeping pace with the advance of industry, she will be always able to supply the millions of the human race with products of universal utility, while, with the wide ocean ever open to her seamen, she will for the future as in the past be the trafficker of the earth, the carrier of the world. Nor will British workmen linger behind if, rising to a level with their opportunities and privileges, they will secure for themselves a position suited to their rights and aspirations.

Methinks I see, at no great distance of time, the great volume of the labouring classes slowly, yet surely, by improvement and by emigration, yield to softer influences, waste and intemperance rebuked and vanquished, the wretched hovel and polluted atmosphere no longer sapping the strength and morals of the people. Methinks I see the British labourer in the enjoyment of a fair share of material comfort and intellectual culture, with manners more refined and morals more elevated, leading a laborious and dignified life; and in all public questions exercising an appreciable and wholesome influence.

— Reading No. 11 —

SWEATED WORKERS, 1890[11]

Low prices were fine for workers who could pay them, but there were those whose wages were so low that they

[11] Fifth Report from the Select Committee of the House of Lords on the Sweating System; together with an Appendix and Proceedings of the Committee," *Parliamentary Papers*, 1890, XVII, xlii-xlv.

could hardly stay alive. Among the most publicized of
such workers were those engaged in sweated industries.
Their way of life was explored in a number of novels and
short stories of social protest, and it was investigated by
a Select Committee of the House of Lords. To raise their
standard of living, the Committee urged, among other
things, the formation of trade unions and cooperative
societies.

✓   ✓   ✓

CONCLUSIONS AND RECOMMENDATIONS

We have endeavoured to extract from the principal
witnesses a clear idea of what they understood by the
term "sweating."

The replies received were neither clear nor con-
sistent. It was urged by some that sweating is an abuse
of the sub-contract system, and consequently that there
can be no sweating where there is no sub-contracting.
Others, on the contrary, maintained that sub-contracting is by no means a necessary element of sweating,
which consists, according to them, in taking advantage
of the necessities of the poorer and more helpless class
of workers, either by forcing them to work too hard or
too long, or under insanitary conditions, or for "starvation wages," or by exacting what some witnesses call
"an undue profit" out of their labour.

Mr. Arnold White observes, that the broadest definition
he can give to the term sweating is the "grinding the faces
of the poor."

We do not propose to enter upon any discussion of the
various definitions placed before us.

It is enough to say that we considered our inquiry
should embrace—

 I. The means employed to take advantage of the necessities of the poorer and more helpless class of
  workers.

 II. The conditions under which such workers live.

 III. The causes that have conduced to the state of
  things disclosed.

 IV. The remedies proposed.

Such having been the scope of our inquiry, and ample evidence having been brought before us on every matter comprised within its scope, we are of opinion that, although we cannot assign an exact meaning to "sweating," the evils known by that name are shown in the foregoing pages of the Report to be—

1. A rate of wages inadequate to the necessities of the workers or disproportionate to the work done.
2. Excessive hours of labour.
3. The insanitary state of the houses in which the work is carried on.

These evils can hardly be exaggerated.

The earnings of the lowest classes of workers are barely sufficient to sustain existence.

The hours of labour are such as to make the lives of the workers periods of almost ceaseless toil, hard and often unhealthy.

The sanitary conditions under which the work is conducted are not only injurious to the health of the persons employed, but are dangerous to the public, especially in the case of the trades concerned in making clothes, as infectious diseases are spread by the sale of garments made in rooms inhabited by persons suffering from small-pox and other diseases.

We make the above statements on evidence of the truth of which we are fully satisfied, and we feel bound to express our admiration of the courage with which the sufferers endure their lot, of the absence of any desire to excite pity by exaggeration, and of the almost unbounded charity they display towards each other in endeavouring by gifts of food and other kindnesses to alleviate any distress for the time being greater than their own.

As a rule, however, it must be remembered that the observations made with respect to sweating apply, in the main, to unskilled or only partially skilled workers, as the thoroughly skilled workers can almost always obtain adequate wages.

When we come to consider the causes of and the remedies for the evils attending the conditions of labour which go under the name of sweating, we are immediately involved in a labyrinth of difficulties. First, we are told that the introduction of sub-contractors or middlemen is the cause of the misery. Undoubtedly, it appears to us that employers are regardless of the moral obligations which attach to capital when they take contracts to supply articles and know nothing of the condition of the workers by whom such articles are made, leaving to a sub-contractor the duty of selecting the workers and giving him by way of compensation a portion of the profit. But it seems to us that the middleman is the consequence, not the cause of the evil; the instrument, not the hand which gives motion to the instrument, which does the mischief. Moreover, the middleman is found to be absent in many cases in which the evils complained of abound.

Further, we think that undue stress has been laid on the injurious effect on wages caused by foreign immigration, inasmuch as we find that the evils complained of obtain in trades, which do not appear to be affected by foreign immigration.

We are of opinion, however, that certain trades are, to some extent, affected by the presence of poor foreigners, for the most part Russian and Polish Jews. These Jews are not charged with immorality or with vice of any description, though represented by some witnesses as being uncleanly in their persons and habits. On the contrary, they are represented on all hands as thrifty and industrious, and they seldom or never come on the rates, as the Jews support by voluntary contributions all their indigent members. What is shown is that the Jewish immigrants can live on what would be starvation wages to Englishmen, that they work for a number of hours almost incredible in length, and that until of late they have not easily lent themselves to trade combinations.

Machinery, by increasing the sub-division of labour, and consequently affording great opportunities for the introduction of unskilled labour is also charged with being a cause of sweating. The answer to this charge seems to be, that in some of the largest clothing and other factories in which labour is admitted to be carried on under favourable conditions to the workers, machinery, and sub-division of labour to the greatest possible extent, are found in every department of the factory.

With more truth it may be said that the inefficiency of

many of the lower class of workers, early marriages, and
the tendency of the residuum of the population in large
towns to form a helpless community, together with a low
standard of life and the excessive supply of unskilled
labour, are the chief factors in producing sweating. Moreover, a large supply of cheap female labour is available in
consequence of the fact that married women working at
unskilled labour in their homes, in the intervals of attend-
ance on their domestic duties and not wholly supporting
themselves, can afford to work at what would be starvation wages to unmarried women. Such being the conditions of the labour market, abundant materials exist to
supply an unscrupulous employer with workers helplessly
dependent upon him.

The most important question is, whether any remedy
can be found for this unhappy state of a portion of the
labouring class. With respect to the low wages and excessive hours of labour, we think that good may be effected
by the extension of coöperative societies, and by well-
considered combination amongst the workers. We are
aware that home-workers form a great obstacle in the way
of combination, inasmuch as they cannot readily be
brought to combine for the purpose of raising wages. To
remove this obstacle we have been urged to recommend
the prohibition by legislation of working at home, but we
think such a measure would be arbitrary and oppressive,
not sanctioned by any precedent in existing law, and impossible to be effectually enforced. . . .

We cannot conclude without expressing our earnest
hope that the exposure of the evils which have been
brought to our notice will induce capitalists to pay closer
attention to the conditions under which the labour which
supplies them with goods is conducted. When legislation
has reached the limit up to which it is effective, the real
amelioration of conditions must be due to increased sense
of responsibility in the employer and improved habits in
the employed. We have reason to think that the present
inquiry itself has not been without moral effect. And we
believe that public attention and public judgment can
effectually check operations in which little regard is shown
to the welfare of work people and to the quality of production, and can also strongly second the zealous and

judicious efforts now being made to encourage thrift, promote temperance, improve dwellings, and raise the tone of living.

— Reading No. 12 —

TRADE UNIONISM: FOR AND AGAINST, 1894 [12]

Late Victorian workers often ascribed the improvement in their standard of living to the activities of trade unions in their behalf. Employers, on the other hand, not infrequently saw in trade unionism a main cause of the great depression. Both positions were vigorously defended by witnesses who appeared before one of the most industrious investigating bodies in English parliamentary history, the Royal Commission on Labour.

✔   ✔   ✔

The employers who have given evidence have usually recognised a legitimate province for trade unions in bargaining as to wages and hours and watching over the general interests of their members, and admitted that strong organisations, acting within those limits, tend on the whole to improve industrial relations, and to make their members act in a better informed way and a more reasonable spirit. . . . But the view has also been put forward, even by those who hold these opinions, that the action

[12] "Fifth and Final Report of the Royal Commission on Labour, Part I," *Parliamentary Papers,* 1894, XXXV, 33-34.

and rules of trade unions have been in some respects
prejudicial to the efficiency of production and to the industrial prosperity of the country.

The allegations upon this point are as follows:—

1. That trade unions have a growing tendency to interfere with details of business, and so to take away
   that concentration of command which is necessary
   for successful management, and hamper employers
   in carrying on their business according to the methods which they believe to be best.

2. That trade unions often misjudge the true position of
   affairs, and by ill-timed and excessive demands, as
   well as by placing employers under apprehension of
   these, discourage enterprise and further investment
   of capital in this country, to the detriment of all
   concerned, including ultimately, if not immediately,
   their own members. As a proof that trade unions
   have done less than is frequently believed in the way
   of raising wages, it is contended that wages have in
   many cases risen as much and as fast in unorganised
   as in organised employments. It is urged that the
   extension of machinery in manufactures, and the development of railways and steam navigation, are the
   main causes of the increased demand for labour and
   consequent advance of wages during the last half
   century.

3. That though organisations may tend to diminish the
   frequency of industrial conflicts, they extend their
   range; and that such conflicts on a large scale, especially in industries which supply raw material, are
   far more injurious to associated and dependent
   trades than are more frequent conflicts on a small
   scale.

4. That workmen with a powerful union behind them
   are apt to become too confident as to their position,
   and to think that they cannot be discharged or punished, and so are likely to become indolent, careless
   or insubordinate, especially in cases where the fore-
   men are unionists with divided allegiance.

5. That the action of trade unions has a tendency to
   bring about a uniformity of wages and hours, both

as between individual workmen and as between different localities; and that by insisting on a minimum wage which, in effect, determines the standard, and by seeking to abolish overtime and piece work, they are reducing workmen to a dead level of enterprise, discouraging work of more than average merit, and taking away from individual workmen the motive power of ambition and self-interest. A few independent workmen, in evidence, concurred with this view, which was put forward by many employers in trades where the unions are most powerful. It is further alleged that the uniformity of wages and hours which trade unions sometimes enforce as between different localities, tends to injure localities possessing less natural advantages in favour of those possessing greater ones, because the former places can only compete with the latter by means of lower wages (usually compensated for by lower cost of living) or longer hours.

6. That trade unions injure trades by the rigidity of their rules. It was said, for instance, that if, at the commencement of the iron ship-building industry, the workmen had enforced their present rigid limitations on apprenticeship, the industry, for want of sufficient hands, could never have developed to its present dimensions. It is also pointed out that the rigid organisation of the different trades in some cases gives rise to a too complete division of work, which prevents men from doing work for which they are qualified and which would at times conveniently fall to their lot, thus occasioning bad economy in production. This was the cause of the recent "demarcation" disputes between various trades in the North of England. In the case of some trades connected with shipbuilding, it was alleged by representatives of "unskilled labourers" employed in them, and admitted by those of the skilled workmen, that the organisation of the latter, as a rule, makes it difficult for those men who start in the lower class to rise to the higher kind of work, even if they have acquired sufficient experience and skill. The rule or

practice of refusing to work with non-unionists may
also be mentioned under this head.

The representatives of trade unions claim that, even
supposing it to be possible to prove some drawbacks, the
existence of these societies is essential to preserve the independence of workmen and to protect their interests. In
proof of the benefits of trade unionism they point to the
position of workmen in various trades before and after
these associations were formed, and maintain that the
action of trade unions has secured improved wages, hours
and conditions of labour not only directly for organised
workmen, but indirectly for those not organised. The refusal of unionists to work with non-unionists is often justified on the ground that the latter without cost to themselves have reaped the benefits secured by the sacrifices
and exertions of the organised workmen.

These witnesses deny that their organisations tend to
enforce a dead level of wages, except with regard to
"minimum rates," and represent that in almost every trade
there are found many men in receipt of wages above what
is known as the "minimum of the trade," in consequence
of their being better workmen. They deny, then, that
these organisations take away the motive of self-interest
and therefore diminish the energy of the individual workman, but they allege that, in the interests of large bodies
of workmen, it is necessary to some extent to restrain by
rules the natural desire of the individual workman to
work overtime, for the sake of higher wages, and other
modes by which he might seek to benefit himself at the
cost of his fellow workmen as well as of his own health
and strength, or that of his offspring. This action is not,
they maintain, injurious in the long run to the general interests of industry, inasmuch as association raises the
"*morale*" of the employed, disciplines and educates them,
and by rendering their work more intelligent, increases
its value. It is necessary, they say, that their rules shall
place a check upon the natural temptation of the employers to excessive competition with one another at the expense of the employed, by way of cheapness of goods and
speed of production attained by overwork and under-pay,
but on the whole, and in the long run, these rules, by

their steadying effect, are good for the trade of the country. They allege that the action of strong trade unions is beneficial even to employers by preventing them from destroying each other through unlimited competition. It is usually admitted on both sides that strong organisations have been proved by experience to be almost a condition precedent to the success of voluntary methods or institutions of conciliation and arbitration, so far as these institutions extend beyond the limits of a single establishment to a whole trade or district, and will be no less essential for the purpose of any further development of such institutions, whether voluntary or created by the action of the State.

— Reading No. 13 —

THE DOCTRINES OF THE LIBERTY AND PROPERTY DEFENCE LEAGUE, 1885 [13]

The great depression encouraged different elements in the English population to urge the government to do something to improve their position, but state intervention alarmed individualists who believed that government meddling would only make things worse. The individualists organized the Liberty and Property Defence League,

[13] *Self Help v. State Help, Speeches Delivered at the Third Annual Meeting of the Liberty and Property Defence League* (London, 1885), pp. 24-29.

whose main purpose was to educate the English public in the glories of self-help and the dangers of state help.

✓   ✓   ✓

Lord Wemyss then said: We have received letters of regret from many important persons who have been unable to attend this meeting. One is from Mr. Pochin, who was once the Liberal member for Stafford, who has taken a great interest in this Association, and who made a most effective speech at the first meeting in this room when the League was formed. He says in his letter:—"I feel more and more satisfied that the League is holding up the right principles of government, and such as must ultimately be accepted, however much such principles may be for the moment departed from by the leaders of parties." I wish to say as Chairman of the Council of the League, of which Lord Pembroke is a member, that we are very grateful to him for the able address he has given us, and for the admirable way in which he has put before this meeting—and, I hope, before the country through the gentlemen who were busy taking down his words—the sound principles which guide this League and the necessity there is, owing to the bad principles there are abroad in matters of legislation—for the existence of such a body as this.

It is now three years since this League was founded. What I and those who had to do with founding the League felt then was that in this country it generally takes about three years to tell whether any movement is or is not likely to succeed. I said to our Secretary, Mr. Crofts, to whose exertions we are so much indebted—for I am bound to say that an abler, more zealous, more effective Secretary no society ever had than the Liberty and Property Defence League possesses in Mr. Crofts—I said to him, "I believe the principle of this League to be absolutely sound, and its existence to be necessary; we shall know in three years whether we can keep it going; in three years we shall know—to use a common expression—whether it is to be a man or a mouse. My conviction is that it is now not only not a mouse, but a man shortly to have gigantic proportions, which I hope will be exercised wholly irrespective of party considerations, solely for the public good, and with the object of keeping both sides in the straight old lines that have made England prosperous and free.

This is my conviction, and I can give you no better proof of it than by asking you to look at our report, which is a model in itself, and which, though it occupies only a sheet of letter paper, contains a great deal and will be found to be pleasant reading by those who take an interest in the League's operations. I will explain what our main object was in forming this organisation—what we expected. In this country, almost every great interest—whether the railways, ships, mines, manufactures, water companies, professions, miscellaneous trades, &c.—have their defensive associations. Now the State does not attack them all at once. It attacks them in detail, and any one of them alone is not strong enough to resist any undue State interference. But by being federated for mutual defence, when the water companies, railways, shipping, or any other interest is attacked, by the combined action of all they can prove themselves stronger than the State, and the State will by and by give up wasting public time in even attempting to plunder any set of men. We are anxious to have as many individual members as possible connected with this society; but our main scheme is the federation of existing bodies constituted for the defence of particular interests, and the securing of a combined general movement of resistance to undue State interference, which, in other words, is State robbery—the robbery of the rich and of the few, in order to bribe and get the votes of the many. That is what it really means.

Look at the success we have achieved within three years! Turn to the paragraph at the bottom of the report headed "Corporate Members." It says: "The means upon which the League has from the outset mainly relied for carrying its principles into effect, namely a working coalition of the defence associations and corporate bodies of the various interests of the country against the attacks of State Socialism upon their property and rights of self-government, have developed beyond expectation. The number of such bodies now in federation with the League is fifty-seven, having doubled within the last year.

Amongst those who have joined this year are some of the chief City Livery Companies." What has brought us the City Companies? It is the introduction of a Bill in the House of Commons by Sir Charles Dilke, which is called—there is a mystery about the name—"The Corporate Property Security Bill."

Now let me interpret: the security of property here meant is not the securing of the property to those to whom it belongs, but the securing it in a way that the owners shall not be allowed to part with it until somebody else obtains it; the transfer to be effected by another Bill next Session in the new Parliament. That is what its so-called security of property amounts to. Well, seven of the large, besides several of the smaller City Companies —eleven altogether—have joined the League. And, in addition, "all the Metropolitan Water Companies, and the Provincial Water Companies' Association, of which there are altogether in the country some 230 conducted by private enterprise. Steps are being taken to develop still further the Parliamentary coöperation of the bodies federated with the League, in collective resistance to the measures of overlegislation by which they are in turn severally threatened. An apt occasion for insisting on this principle has arisen in connection with the 'Corporate Property Security Bill,' introduced this session, of which advantage has been taken by the League, and with marked results. Its success in combining opposition to this Bill may be measured by the virulence with which the League and its utterances have been attacked in various quarters."

I merely read this to show that this League in the three years of its existence has liberated a spring of political action which is abundant, and which I hope will cause such a flood as will sweep away, in the course of time, all attempts at State interference in the business transactions of life in the case of every Briton of every class. We know in the long run what State interference means. No nation can prosper with undue state interference, and unless its people are allowed to manage their own affairs in their own way, and that is the object which this League seeks to attain wholly irrespective of party spirit; and, I am glad to see here to-day men of all shades of political opinion, and of various occupations in life, for, I believe, we have working men present amongst us. As Chairman of the Council, I heartily congratulate members of the League upon the success which has attended its efforts, and I believe those efforts will succeed in the future even more than they have done in the past. This is our report, which I, as Chairman of the Council, present to this Meeting.

— Reading No. 14 —

THE MENACE OF SOCIALISM, 1890 [14]

Individualists were convinced that human nature required that people be let alone. If the government interfered in the affairs of its citizens, the results would be disastrous. People would get lazy, and the energetic would find their incentive crushed. In short, the wealth of the nation would diminish and its character would degenerate.

✓   ✓   ✓

Major Creswell: My lords, ladies, and gentlemen, I have the honour to move, "That the Report of the progress and work of the League during the past year, presented by the Council, be adopted." I do not think many words from me are necessary in moving this resolution, as you have already heard the policy of the League explained by its President (Lord Wemyss), you have also, I

[14] David Dudley Field, *The Duties of the State: An Address* (London, 1890), pp. 25-27.

may take it, been furnished with a copy of the Report, and you have had the privilege of hearing the grand address delivered by the Honourable David Dudley Field. In that address he has pictured to you exactly the true foundation of the State, and has accurately defined its function. Now, the object of this League is to uphold individual liberty and the true function of the State, and I hope it will continue to exist and flourish for that purpose. Individual liberty is, I will not say the corner stone but the foundation stone of the entire fabric of our whole social life. You will see by this Report that the work of the League has been very great indeed. It has engaged the attention not only of the Press, but of lecturers and special agents all over the country. Why is this? Because, as has been alleged, property is attacked and threatened, and capital lacks confidence in investments. Confidence is disappearing, and why? Because of the poisonous views of socialists and demagogues which are so loudly and frequently enunciated. I should like to know, would electricity, the great inventions of chemistry and other beneficent inventions have existed in the present day if socialism had had its way in this country in the past? No. It is to individualism, to the certainty that a man will reap the full reward of his risk and enterprise, if successful, that we owe these things. A man spends, say thousands of pounds—a quarter of a million—in carrying out an invention that will benefit the world. He risks the whole of his money upon his idea to the possible disadvantage of himself and his family. It would be a serious and unjust thing indeed, if, when success crowned his self-sacrificing effort, he were to be deprived of the full benefit of his enterprise. (*Applause.*)

It has always been a recognised rule that a man who makes himself famous by his deeds shall be rewarded. Where would be the great men of the present, and the great merchants and manufacturers, and traders of this country if they had not been permitted to keep the rewards of their enterprise? The object of this League is to protect private enterprise against the socialistic despoiler, and to encourage the capable. At the same time, I am sure, we all feel it to be our duty to take care of the weak and helpless, those who cannot take care of themselves.

The effect of all this socialism, strikes, and new unionism has been to render capital idle, and, as a consequence, Mr. Goschen has been enabled to reduce the interest on consols from 3% to 2¾ and 2½. There is too much money awaiting secure investment. Capital is cheap. Had it not been for socialistic preaching, trade unionism, and strikes, much more money would have been invested in land and industries, and much more labour would have been employed. Who would invest in land, docks, and houses when all alike were threatened with taxation so heavy as to reduce the net profit to a margin so small as to make it not worth the while of capital to invest? The result will be that, as capital finds less profitable employment, the Chancellor of the Exchequer will be able to reduce the interest on consols another ¼ per cent.; and if things go on as they are now going he would be able to make even further reductions. This League has, I see by this Report, a great work before it. It will be its duty to oppose Bills for increasing the spending powers of two great bodies in the metropolis, whose exactions we already feel very severely. (*Hear, hear.*)

There are other things mentioned in the Report of equal importance. I hope you will adopt the Report in its entirety and not only so, but that you will one and all—if you have not already done so—subscribe to the funds of this League, and induce your friends to become subscribers also. (*Applause.*) Let not the League be crippled in its good and necessary work for want of pecuniary support. For your own sake in the present, and that of your children in the future, and of your children's children, help the League to maintain those institutions which have made this country prosperous in the past and present. We can improve upon the past, but we cannot replace it by anything else. Let us improve our institutions where necessary as we go on, but do not destroy them or set up a god we have not known the benefit of. (*Applause.*)

— Reading No. 15 —

W. H. MALLOCK AND THE OFFENSIVE OF THE INDIVIDUALISTS, 1894 [15]

Next to Herbert Spencer, the towering publicist in the ranks of the individualists was W. H. Mallock. He spoke and wrote a great deal in defense of self-help and in opposition to non-socialist intervention as well as socialism. The following selection is typical of his conception of a fighting conservatism.

↗   ↗   ↗

I was asked, early this autumn, if I would consent to give, during the winter, addresses to Conservative Clubs in various parts of the kingdom. But I found that, owing to circumstances, this would be quite impossible. I regretted much that it should be so; and I regretted it for the following reason. Each Conservative Club is, in its own neighbourhood, a centre of intellectual influence; and whatever knowledge its members may elucidate within doors, they carry away with them for use in the world outside. They use it to strengthen those who agree with them, and to convert or to silence those who do not.

They may be very accurately compared to the rose of an intellectual watering pot, by which sound knowledge and arguments are distributed far and wide. But if this be true—and I think you will admit that in varying degrees it is true—of even small local clubs or associations, where there is any intelligent discussion about political matters at all, much more must it be true of a club, association, or body of men acting together, in a town like London— and especially of a body of men like yourselves, who are not only in close connection with the Conservative Cen-

[15] W. H. Mallock, *Labour as an Agent in the Production of the National Wealth* (London, 1894), pp. 1-2, 22-23.

tral Office, but have connected yourselves with it for the
special purpose of strengthening and widening foundations of Conservatism by the intellectual weapon of argument on public platforms.

For this reason, when I found that I should be unable
to deliver a course of addresses in the country, I asked
Mr. Middleton if it would be possible to arrange a meeting at which I might have the privilege of addressing the
active Conservative speakers of London, for I knew that
if I have anything to say that might be usefully said at
any meeting, in saying it to the speakers of London I
should be saying it to a hundred meetings. Whether what
I shall say will be of any utility at all—that, gentlemen,
must be determined by yourselves. But if it is useful in
this way, then I shall know that in speaking to each one of
you, I have virtually spoken, not to one person, but to
thousands. . . .

We often hear it said that we Conservatives shrink
from argument on social questions. Gentlemen, the more
I consider the matter, the more am I impressed by the
multitude and the keenness of the argumentative weapons
that lie at our feet, if we will only take the trouble to pick
them up and use them. The deeper we go into the consideration of social questions, the more plain does the un-
scientific character of Socialism and Collectivism appear
to us; and the more carefully we go into economic statistics, the more ludicrously and wildly false are the facts
and figures seen to be on which the Socialistic and semi-
Socialistic speakers mainly rely. They have, however, by
some means or other given to these fallacies a practical
power by diffusing them amongst their supporters, so that
they are heard over and over again, whenever a Socialistic
speech is made. It is our duty, it seems to me, to diffuse
the truth with equal energy, so that the same points may
be made over and over again, whenever occasion offers,
in every constituency, on every platform; and I trust you
may agree with me, that one of the first fallacies that
should be attacked in this way is that great fundamental
fallacy as to labour and capital, on which I have dwelt
to-night—the childish fallacy that the labouring classes
are the only, or indeed the chief, producing classes in a
civilisation like our own. I trust you may agree with me

that this childish fallacy should be attacked and exposed
everywhere, by the same facts and arguments, so that the
whole country, if possible, may be made to ring with the
exposure; and few things would give me greater pleasure than to think that what I have said to-night, to so important and influential a body as yourselves, may have
done something to contribute to this result.

— Reading No. 16 —

DISRAELI AND THE HEALTH OF THE PEOPLE, 1872 [16]

The Conservative Party had a long tradition of intervention in behalf of the poor, and Tory leaders like Disraeli believed that the continuation of this tradition was
necessary if the party was to survive in the modern world.
In an important speech in Manchester in 1872 Disraeli
made social welfare legislation a campaign issue. The
victory of the Conservatives two years later was in part
due to his stand on intervention.

✓   ✓   ✓

. . . Our opponents assure us that the Conservative party
have no political programme; and, therefore, they must
look with much satisfaction to one whom you honour
to-night by considering him the leader and representative
of your opinions when he comes forward, at your invita-

[16] T. E. Kebbel, ed., *Selected Speeches of the Late Right
Honourable the Earl of Beaconsfield* (2 vols., London,
1882), II, 491-92, 501-02, 510-12.

tion, to express to you what that programme is. The Conservative party are accused of having no programme of policy. If by a programme is meant a plan to despoil churches and plunder landlords, I admit we have no programme. If by a programme is meant a policy which assails or menaces every institution and every interest, every class and every calling in the country, I admit we have no programme. But if to have a policy with distinct ends, and these such as most deeply interest the great body of the nation, be a becoming programme for a political party, then, I contend, we have an adequate programme, and one which, here or elsewhere, I shall always be prepared to assert and to vindicate.

Gentlemen, the programme of the Conservative party is to maintain the Constitution of the country. I have not come down to Manchester to deliver an essay on the English Constitution; but when the banner of Republicanism is unfurled—when the fundamental principles of our institutions are controverted—I think, perhaps, it may not be inconvenient that I should make some few practical remarks upon the character of our Constitution—upon that monarchy, limited by the co-ordinate authority of Estates of the realm, which, under the title of Queen, Lords and Commons, has contributed so greatly to the prosperity of this country, and with the maintenance of which I believe that prosperity is bound up.

Gentlemen, since the settlement of that Constitution, now nearly two centuries ago, England has never experienced a revolution, though there is no country in which there has been so continuous and such considerable change. How is this? Because the wisdom of your forefathers placed the prize of supreme power without the sphere of human passions. Whatever the struggle of parties, whatever the strife of factions, whatever the excitement and exaltation of the public mind, there has always been something in this country round which all classes and parties could rally, representing the majesty of the law, the administration of justice, and involving, at the same time, the security for every man's rights and the fountain of honour. Now, gentlemen, it is well clearly to comprehend what is meant by a country not having a revolution for two centuries. It means, for that space, the unbroken exercise and enjoyment of the ingenuity of man. It means, for that space, the continuous application of the discoveries of science to his comfort and convenience. It means the accumulation of capital, the elevation of labour, the establishment of those admirable factories which cover your district; the unwearied improvement of the cultivation of the land, which has extracted from a somewhat churlish soil harvests more exuberant than those furnished by lands nearer to the sun. It means the continuous order which is the only parent of personal liberty and political right. And you owe all these, gentlemen, to the Throne. . . .

Lord Grey, in his measure of 1832, which was no doubt a statesmanlike measure, committed a great and for a time it appeared an irretrievable error. By that measure he fortified the legitimate influence of the aristocracy; but he not only made no provision for the representation of the working classes in the Constitution, but he absolutely abolished those ancient franchises which the working classes had peculiarly enjoyed and exercised from time immemorial. Gentlemen, that was the origin of Chartism, and of that electoral uneasiness which existed in this country more or less for thirty years. The Liberal party, I feel it my duty to say, had not acted fairly by this question. In their adversity they held out hopes to the working classes, but when they had a strong Government they laughed their vows to scorn. In 1848 there was a French Revolution and a Republic was established. No one can have forgotten what the effect was in this country. I remember the day when not a woman could leave her house in London, and when cannon were planted on Westminster Bridge. When Lord Derby became Prime Minister affairs had arrived at such a point that it was of the first moment that the question should be sincerely dealt with. He had to encounter great difficulties, but he accomplished his purpose with the support of a united party. And, gentlemen, what has been the result? A year ago there was another revolution in France, and a Republic was again established of the most menacing character. What happened in this country? You could not get half a dozen men to assemble in a street and grumble. Why? Because the people had got what they wanted. They were content and they were grateful. . . .

Gentlemen, I think public attention . . . ought to be concentrated upon sanitary legislation. That is a wide subject, and, if properly treated, comprises almost every consideration which has just claim upon legislative interference. Pure air, pure water, the inspection of unhealthy habitations, the adulteration of food, these and many kindred matters may be legitimately dealt with by the Legislature; and I am bound to say the Legislature is not idle upon them; for we have at this time two important measures before Parliament on the subject. One—by a late colleague of mine, Sir Charles Adderley—is a large and comprehensive measure, founded upon a sure basis, for it consolidates all existing public Acts and improves them. A prejudice has been raised against that proposal, by stating that it interferes with the private Acts of the great towns. I take this opportunity of contradicting that. The Bill of Sir Charles Adderley does not touch the Acts of the great towns. It only allows them if they think fit to avail themselves of its new provisions.

The other measure, by the government, is of a partial character. What it comprises is good, so far as it goes, but it shrinks from that bold consolidation of existing Acts which I think one of the great merits of Sir Charles Adderley's Bill, which permits us to become acquainted with how much may be done in favour of sanitary improvement by existing provisions. Gentlemen, I cannot impress upon you too strongly my conviction of the importance of the Legislature and society uniting together in favour of these important results. A great scholar and a great wit, 300 years ago, said that, in his opinion, there was a great mistake in the Vulgate, which as you all know is the Latin translation of the Holy Scriptures, and that instead of saying "Vanity of vanities, all is vanity"—*Vanitas vanitatum, omnia vanitas*—the wise and witty King really said *Sanitas sanitatum, omnia sanitas*. Gentlemen, it is impossible to overrate the importance of the subject. After all, the first consideration of a minister should be the health of the people. A land may be covered with historic trophies, with museums of science and galleries of

art, with universities and with libraries; the people may be
civilised and ingenious; the country may be even famous
in the annals and action of the world, but, gentlemen, if
the population every ten years decreases, and the stature
of the race every ten years diminishes, the history of that
country will soon be the history of the past. . . .

— Reading No. 17 —

LORD RANDOLPH CHURCHILL'S TORY DEMOCRACY, 1883[17]

In 1880 the Conservatives were defeated, and shortly
afterwards Lord Beaconsfield (Disraeli) died. The unveil-
ing in 1883 of a statue in his memory provided the young
Tory leader, Lord Randolph Churchill, with an opportunity to reassess the legacy of Disraeli and reassert the need
for Tory Democracy. Churchill saw in state intervention
the salvation of his party and the cure of the depression.

✓   ✓   ✓

. . . on the 19th April, 1881, the mischievous and evil-
minded fortune which had persecuted the Tories sent a
crowning blow, and Lord Beaconsfield passed away.

From that hour to this there has hardly been a Tory in
or out of Parliament, high or low, rich or poor, who, ob-
serving at any particular moment the political situation,
has not exclaimed, muttered, or thought, "Oh, if Lord

[17] Lord Randolph S. Churchill, "Elijah's Mantle; April 19th,
1883," *The Fortnightly Review*, n.s., XXXIII (1883),
614-16, 621.

Beaconsfield were alive!" This is really the proudest monument to the departed leader, more enduring than the bronze on the Abbey Green. This is the truest testimony of his inestimable value to the party who for so long jeered, feared, flouted, followed, and following at the last greatly loved. This, too, is the criticism pointed and unanswerable on the conduct of affairs since his death, which no amount of memorials of confidence, no number of dinners in Pall Mall, no repetitions, however frequent, of gushing embraces between the lord and the commoner, can meet, modify, or gainsay.

Such must have been the train of thought, or something very similar, which impressed the chief actors in the ceremony that marked the 19th of April, 1883, judging from the utterances of which they delivered themselves. It is remarkable that in the speeches which were made on that occasion not one spark of hope or cheerfulness can be detected. Artificial eulogies, vapid adjectives, gloomy recollections were the order of the day. Yet the career of Lord Beaconsfield was rich in illustrations which, if felicitously treated, might have stimulated those who heard, and those who read, to renewed efforts, fresh enthusiasm, unlimited confidence in the performance of the laborious task of resistance to the triumphant hosts of Radicalism and Demagogy. His life may be painted in a sentence: Failure, failure, failure, partial success, renewed failure, ultimate and complete triumph. The disasters of 1880 may be greatly overestimated in learning the lesson of Lord Beaconsfield's career. It is not foolish to assume that, if Lord Beaconsfield in 1874 had been the same man who turned out Mr. Gladstone in 1866, the Tory party would be in office now. But he was very old and very worn when he got to the top of the tree, and he was but indifferently served by some of his colleagues. Advancing years, an enfeebled constitution, a singularly exhausting and painful form of disease, had compelled him to give way to a disposition naturally indolent, unsuited to the constant mastery of dry administrative detail. He must often have thought that he had done nearly enough, that he might with justice allow himself to seek in the distractions of London society a pleasure and a repose to which, during most of his life, he had been a stranger.

Only the most captious mind could blame him for this, but this it was nevertheless which greatly conduced to the downfall of his Government. What time he gave to public affairs was absorbed in studying, with the assistance of the Foreign Secretary, the various phases of the Eastern complication. All else was neglected. Finance was left entirely to the Chancellor of the Exchequer, in whose unaided hands deficits and floating debts grew apace. The other heads of departments were all allowed to go their own way, doing what seemed good in their eyes. There was no master-mind pervading and controlling every branch of the administration. Election affairs and organization went to the dogs. The care, the experience, the personal supervision which Mr. Disraeli, assisted by a few practised hands, had bestowed upon the preparations for the general election of 1874 disappeared. A weak but wide-spreading centralization enervated the vigour of the provincial organization. A stupefying degree of over-confidence, a foolish contempt for the adversary, a fatally erroneous estimate of the revived influence of Mr. Gladstone—these causes, and these alone, all of them preventible, slowly but surely worked the ruin. A golden opportunity had been given to the Tories, but, owing to the natural decay of Lord Beaconsfield's physical vigour, the opportunity was wasted and lost. Who shall say whether such an opportunity will ever return? The Liberals can afford better to sustain great disasters than the Conservatives, for there is a recuperative power innate in Liberal principles—the result of the longing of the human mind for progress and for adventure—which enables them to recover rapidly and unexpectedly from misfortunes which would seem to be fatal. The Tories, though possessing many other advantages, fail in this respect. As time goes on their successes will be fewer and separated from each other by intervals of growing length; unless, indeed, the policy and the principles of the Tory party should undergo a surprising development; unless the secret of Lord Beaconsfield's theory of government is appropriated, understood, believed in, sown broadcast amongst the people; unless the mantle of Elijah should fall upon some one who is capable enough and fortunate enough, carrying with him a united party, to bring to perfection those schemes of imperial rule, of social reform which Lord Beaconsfield had only time to dream of, to hint at, and to sketch. . . .

Some of Lord Beaconsfield's phrases will bear any amount of microscopic examination. Speaking at Manchester in 1871 [sic], by the alteration of a letter in a quotation from the Vulgate, he revealed the policy which ought to guide Tory leaders at the present time: *"Sanitas sanitatum, omnia sanitas."* Such was the quotation in which a careful mind will discover a scheme of social progress and reform, of dimensions so large and wide-spreading that many volumes would not suffice to explain its details. By it is shadowed forth, and in it is embraced, a social revolution which, passing by and diverting attention from wild longings for organic change, commences with the little piddling Boards of Health which occupy and delight the Local Government Department, comprises Lord Salisbury's plans for the amelioration of the dwellings of the poor, carries with it Lord Carnarvon's ideal of compulsory national insurance, includes Sir Wilfrid Lawson's temperance propaganda, preserves and reclaims commons and open spaces favoured by Mr. Bryce, constructs people's parks, collects and opens to the masses museums, libraries, art-galleries, does not disdain the public washhouses of Mr. Jesse Collings. Public and private thrift must animate the whole, for it is from public thrift that the funds for these largesses can be drawn, and it is by private thrift alone that their results can be utilised and appreciated. The expression "Tory Democracy" has excited the wonder of some, the alarm of others, and great and bitter ridicule from the Radical party. It has, unfortunately, been subjected to some discredit by having been used by Mr. Forwood, the Conservative candidate at the last Liverpool election, who used it without knowing what he was talking about. But the "Tory Democracy" may yet exist; the elements for its composition only require to be collected, and the labour may some day possibly be effected by the man, whoever

he may be, upon whom the mantle of Elijah has
descended.

— Reading No. 18 —

JOSEPH CHAMBERLAIN: SCOURGE OF THE INDIVIDUALISTS, 1885 [18]

Randolph Churchill's social ideas were remarkably
similar to those of Joseph Chamberlain. Just as Churchill
frightened his fellow-Conservatives, so Chamberlain
frightened his fellow-Liberals. As far as most of their
colleagues were concerned, both were Socialists. In fact,
however, they saw in state intervention in behalf of the
poor a way to stop socialism.

✓   ✓   ✓

Domestic Legislation
(At Hull, August 5, 1885)

It is not desirable, even if it were possible, that all
Liberals should think exactly alike, and that every candidate should be cut to precisely the same pattern. In the
Liberal army there must be pioneers to clear the way, and
there must be men who watch the rear. Some may always
be in advance, others may occasionally lag behind; but
the only thing we have a right to demand is, that no one
shall stand still, and that all should be willing to follow
the main lines of Liberal progress to which the whole

[18] Henry W. Lucy, ed., *Speeches of the Right Hon. Joseph
Chamberlain, M.P.* (London, 1885), pp. 161-64.

party are committed. I do not conceal from you my own opinion that the pace will be a little faster in the future than it has been in the past. Everywhere the reforms to which the resolution has made reference are casting their shadows before. Everywhere in the country I see a quickening of political life. Everywhere there is discussion, and hope, and expectation. Gentlemen, it will be dangerous to disappoint that hope. It will be impossible to stifle that discussion; and if there are any people who imagine that the enfranchisement of two millions of citizens can have taken place, and that these men intend to make no use of the privilege which has been conferred upon them, they will have a rude awakening. These are not wise men, believe me—they are not the true friends of the institutions of this country who will not bring impartial minds to the consideration of the new problems that are calling for solution.

A HOPEFUL FUTURE.

I am not altogether surprised, under these circumstances, that there has recently been a demand in some quarters that the leaders of the two great parties should frame a definite programme; that they should discard empty platitudes and generalities, and put a clear issue before the electors. I can say for myself personally that I have done my best in that direction; and although in the speeches I have recently made I have disclaimed any right to speak for the party as a whole, I have been soundly rated for my presumption in daring to speak at all, and I have been solemnly excommunicated by some of the great authorities who claim a monopoly of the orthodox Liberal faith and doctrine. Gentlemen, I am not discouraged; I am not repentant. I am told if I pursue this course that I shall break up the party, and that I shall altogether destroy any chance which I might otherwise have had of office. I do not believe it. But if it were true I say that I care little for party, and nothing at all for office, except so far as these things may be made instrumental in promoting the objects which I publicly avowed when I first entered Parliament, and which I will prosecute so long as I remain in public life. The Liberal party has always seemed to me the great agency of progress and reform, and by the changes which have recently taken place it has secured a vantage ground which I myself had hardly ever dared to anticipate. I had looked forward with hope to the future, but I had not supposed in my time so great a change could have been successfully effected. But now that my wildest expectations have been surpassed, I am not willing to be silent as to the uses to which I believe the people ought to put the new power and the privileges which have been conferred upon them. I had already a deep conviction that when the people came to govern themselves, and when the clamour of vested interests and class privileges was overborne by the powerful voice of the whole nation, that then the social evils which disgrace our civilization and the wrongs which have cried vainly for redress would at last find a hearing and a remedy. And if that be not so it will be no longer statesmen or Governments that you will have to blame. It will not be the fault of parties or of individuals; it will be the apathy or the ignorance, the indifference or the folly of the people themselves which alone can hinder their progress and their prosperity.

NOT TO ABASE THE RICH, BUT TO UPLIFT THE POOR.

One of the speakers has said, and said truly, that this is a critical time; it is the turning-point of our political history; and if the people are content with the old formulae, and with the watchwords which satisfied a limited electorate, then I think some of us might have been better employed than we were when we joined the agitation of last autumn, and the enfranchisement of two millions of men will have been a barren and an unprofitable business. We shall have perfected the machinery, but we shall have done nothing at all to improve the manufacture. I do not want you to think that I suggest to you that legislation can accomplish all that we desire, and, above all, I would not lead you into wild and revolutionary projects, which would upset unnecessarily the existing order of things. But, on the other hand, I want you not to accept as final or as perfect, arrangements under which hundreds of thousands, nay, millions, of your fellow-countrymen are subjected to untold privations and misery, with the evidence all around them of accumulated wealth and unbounded luxury.

The extremes of wealth and of poverty are alike the sources of great temptation. I believe that the great evil with which we have to deal is the excessive inequality in the distribution of riches. Ignorance, intemperance, immorality, and disease—these things are all interdependent and closely connected; and although they are often the cause of poverty, they are still more frequently the consequence of destitution, and if we can do anything to raise the condition of the poor in this country, to elevate the masses of the people, and give them the means of enjoyment and recreation, to afford to them opportunities of improvement, we should do more for the prosperity, ay, for the morality of this country than anything we can do by laws, however stringent, for the prevention of excess, or the prevention of crime. I want you to make this the first object in the Liberal programme for the reformed Parliament.

It is not our duty, it is not our wish, to pull down and abase the rich, although I do not think that the excessive aggregation of wealth in a few hands is any advantage to anybody; but our object is to raise the general condition of the people. The other day I was present at a meeting, when a labourer was called upon suddenly to speak. He got up, and in his rude dialect, without any rhetorical flourish, said something to this effect. He said, "Neighbours and friends, you have known me for forty years. I have lived among you, and worked among you. I am not a drunkard; I am a steady man; I am an industrious man; I am not a spending man. I have worked and laboured for forty years; it has been a weary task, and I ain't any forwarder now than I was when I began. What is the reason of it? What is the remedy?" Gentlemen, believe me, the questions of the poor labourer cannot be put aside. Our ideal, I think, should be that in this rich country, where everything seems to be in profusion, an honest, a decent, and an industrious man should be able to earn a livelihood for himself and his family, should have access to some means of self-improvement and enjoyment, and should be able to lay aside something for sickness and old age. Is that unreasonable? Is it impossible? . . .

I am not a Communist, although some people will have it that I am. Considering the difference in the character and the capacity of men, I do not believe that there can ever be an absolute equality of conditions, and I think that nothing would be more undesirable than that we should remove the stimulus to industry and thrift and exertion which is afforded by the security given to every man in the enjoyment of the fruits of his own individual exertions. I am opposed to confiscation in every shape or form, because I believe that it would destroy that security, and lessen that stimulus. But on the other hand, I am in favour of accompanying the protection which is afforded to property with a large and stringent interpretation of the obligations of property. . . .

— Reading No. 19 —

WILLIAM MORRIS COMPOSES SOCIALIST CHANTS, 1885 [19]

The late Victorian Socialists were very few in number, but they were fortunate in winning to their ranks a goodly number of able writers, whose productivity concealed the smallness of the movement they championed. Of these writers none was so highly regarded as William Morris. It came as a shock to many of his contemporaries that the author of *The Defense of Guenevere, The Life and*

[19] William Morris, *Chants for Socialists* (London, 1885), pp. 3-5.

Death of Jason, and *The Earthly Paradise* was now writing *Chants for Socialists.*

THE DAY IS COMING

Come hither lads, and hearken, for a tale there is to tell,
Of the wonderful days a'coming when all shall be better
    than well.

And the tale shall be told of a country, a land in the midst
    of the sea,
And folk shall call it England in the days that are going
    to be.

There more than one in a thousand in the days that are
    yet to come,
Shall have some hope of the morrow, some joy of the
    ancient home.

For then—laugh not, but listen, to this strange tale of
    mine—
All folk that are in England shall be better lodged than
    swine.

Then a man shall work and bethink him, and rejoice in
    the deeds of his hand,
Nor yet come home in the even too faint and weary to
    stand.

Men in that time a'coming shall work and have no fear
For to-morrow's lack of earning and the hunger-wolf
    anear.

I tell you this for a wonder, that no man then shall be
    glad
Of his fellow's fall and mishap to snatch at the work he
    had.

For that which the worker winneth shall then be his
    indeed,
Nor shall half be reaped for nothing by him that sowed
    no seed.

O strange new wonderful justice! But for whom shall
we gather the gain?
For ourselves and for each of our fellows, and no hand
shall labour in vain.

Then all *mine* and all *thine* shall be *ours,* and no more
shall any man crave
For riches that serve for nothing but to fetter a friend for
a slave.

And what wealth then shall be left us when none shall
gather gold
To buy his friend in the market, and pinch and pine the
sold?

Nay, what save the lovely city, and the little house on the
hill,
And the wastes and the woodland beauty, and the happy
fields we till.

And the homes of ancient stories, the tombs of the
mighty dead;
And the wise men seeking out marvels, and the poet's
teeming head;

And the painter's hand of wonder; and the marvellous
fiddle-bow,
And the banded choirs of music:—all those that do and
know.

For all these shall be ours and all men's, nor shall any
lack a share
Of the toil and the gain of living in the days when the
world grows fair.

Ah! such are the days that shall be! But what are the
deeds of to-day,
In the days of the years we dwell in, that wear our lives
away?

Why, then, and for what are we waiting? There are three
words to speak.

WE WILL IT, and what is the foeman but the dream-
strong wakened and weak?

O why and for what are we waiting? while our brothers
droop and die,
And on every wind of the heavens a wasted life goes by.

How long shall they reproach us where crowd on crowd
they dwell,
Poor ghosts of the wicked city, the gold-crushed hungry
hell?

Through squalid life they laboured, in sordid grief they
died,
Those sons of a mighty mother, those props of England's
pride.

They are gone; there is none can undo it, nor save our
souls from the curse;
But many a million cometh, and shall they be better or
worse?

It is we must answer and hasten, and open wide the door
For the rich man's hurrying terror, and the slow-foot
hope of the poor.

Yea, the voiceless wrath of the wretched, and their un-
learned discontent,
We must give it voice and wisdom till the waiting-tide be
spent.

Come, then, since all things call us, the living and the
dead,
And o'er the weltering tangle a glimmering light is shed.

Come, then, let us cast off fooling, and put by ease and
rest,
For the CAUSE alone is worthy till the good days bring
the best.

Come, join in the only battle wherein no man can fail,
Where whoso fadeth and dieth, yet his deed shall still
prevail.

Ah! come, cast off all fooling, for this, at least, we know:
That the Dawn and the Day is coming, and forth the
   Banners go.

— Reading No. 20 —

THE BASIS OF THE FABIAN SOCIETY, 1887[20]

No late Victorian Socialist organization has received
so much attention as the Fabian Society. Mainly this is
because it attracted in its early years a remarkable number of young men and women who were to achieve
eminence in later times in a variety of fields. To keep
these people in a group was a major problem. Not surprisingly, therefore, the "Basis" or Constitution that
served the Society from 1887 until the end of World War
I had to be kept vague.

✓   ✓   ✓

The Fabian Society consists of Socialists.

It therefore aims at the reorganisation of Society by the
emancipation of Land and Industrial Capital from individual and class ownership, and the vesting of them in the
community for the general benefit. In this way only can
the natural and acquired advantages of the country be
equitably shared by the whole people.

The Society accordingly works for the extinction of
private property in Land and of the consequent indi-

[20] Edward R. Pease, *The History of the Fabian Society* (London, rev. ed., 1926), p. 284.

vidual appropriation, in the form of Rent, of the price paid for permission to use the earth, as well as for the advantages of superior soils and sites.

The Society, further, works for the transfer to the community of the administration of such industrial Capital as can conveniently be managed socially. For, owing to the monopoly of the means of production in the past, industrial inventions and the transformation of surplus income into Capital have mainly enriched the proprietary class, the worker being now dependent on that class for leave to earn a living.

If these measures be carried out, without compensation (though not without such relief to expropriated individuals as may seem fit to the community), Rent and Interest will be added to the reward of labour, the idle class now living on the labour of others will necessarily disappear, and practical equality of opportunity will be maintained by the spontaneous action of economic forces with much less interference with personal liberty than the present system entails.

For the attainment of these ends the Fabian Society looks to the spread of Socialist opinions, and the social and political changes consequent thereon, *including the establishment of equal citizenship for men and women.* [The words in italics were added in 1907.] It seeks to achieve these ends by the general dissemination of knowledge as to the relation between the individual and Society in its economic, ethical, and political aspects.

ROBERT BLATCHFORD'S *MERRIE ENGLAND*, 1894 [21]

No Socialist book in the late Victorian period reached such a large audience as Robert Blatchford's *Merrie England*. Its purpose was to convince workers that as long as capitalism continued they would suffer from unemployment, low wages, and lack of leisure. Blatchford's appeal was ethical and patriotic as well as economic.

✦ ✦ ✦

Socialism!

John Smith, do you know what Socialism is? You have heard it denounced many a time, and it is said that you do not believe in it; but do you know what it is?

Good or bad, wise or foolish, it is all I have to offer as a remedy for the many evils of which I have been complaining.

Good or bad, wise or foolish, Socialism is the only remedy in sight. None of its opponents, none of your friends, the members of Parliament, old trade union leaders, Tory and Liberal editors, parsons, priests, lawyers, and men of substance have any remedy to offer at all.

Some of them are sorry or profess to be sorry, that there is so much misery in the land; some of them offer a little mild charity, some a little feeble legislation, but there is no great radical cure to be heard of except Socialism.

What is Socialism? I am going to tell you, and I ask you to listen patiently, and to judge fairly. You have heard Socialism reviled by speakers and writers. You know that the Pope has denounced it, and that the Bishop

[21] Robert Blatchford, *Merrie England* (London, 1894), pp. 98-102.

of Manchester has denounced it. You know that men like Herbert Spencer, Charles Bradlaugh, and John Morley have written and spoken against it, and doubtless you have got an idea that it is as unworthy, as unwise, and as unworkable as such men say it is. Now I will describe it for you and you shall draw your own conclusions.

But before I tell you what Socialism is, I must tell you what Socialism is not. For half our time as champions of Socialism is wasted in denials of false descriptions of Socialism; and to a large extent the anger, the ridicule, and the argument of the opponents of Socialism are hurled against a Socialism which has no existence except in their own heated minds.

Socialism does not consist in violently seizing upon the property of the rich and sharing it out amongst the poor.

Socialists do not propose by a single Act of Parliament, or by a sudden revolution, to put all men on an equality, and compel them to remain so. Socialism is not a wild dream of a happy land where the apples will drop off the trees into our open mouths, the fish come out of the rivers and fry themselves for dinner, and the looms turn out ready-made suits of velvet with golden buttons without the trouble of coaling the engine. Neither is it a dream of a nation of stained-glass angels, who never say damn, who always love their neighbours better than themselves, and who never need to work unless they wish to.

No, Socialism is none of those things. It is a scientific scheme of national Government, entirely wise, just, and *practical*. And now let us see.

For convenience sake, Socialism is generally divided into two kinds. These are called—

1. Practical Socialism.
2. Ideal Socialism.

Really they are only part of one whole; Practical Socialism being a kind of preliminary step towards Ideal Socialism, so that we might with more reason call them Elementary and Advanced Socialism.

I am an ideal Socialist, and desire to have the whole Socialistic programme carried out.

Practical Socialism is so simple that a child may

understand it. It is a kind of national scheme of co-opera-
tion, managed by the State. Its programme consists,
essentially, of one demand, that the land and other instruments of production shall be the common property of
the people, and shall be used and governed by the people
for the people.

Make the land and all the instruments of production
State property; put all farms, mines, mills, ships, railways,
and shops under State control, as you have already put
the postal and telegraphic services under State control,
and Practical Socialism is accomplished.

The postal and telegraphic service is the standing proof
of the capacity of the State to manage the public business
with economy and success.

That which has been done with the post-offices may be
done with mines, trams, railways, and factories.

The difference between Socialism and the state of
things now in existence will now be plain to you.

At present the land—that is, England—does not belong to the people—to the English—but to a few rich
men. The mines, mills, ships, shops, canals, railways,
houses, docks, harbours, and machinery do not belong
to the people, but to a few rich men.

Therefore the land, the factories, the railways, ships,
and machinery are not used for the general good of the
people, but are used to make wealth for the few rich
men who own them. Socialists say that this arrangement
is unjust and unwise, that it entails waste as well as
misery, and that it would be better for all, even for the
rich, that the land and other instruments of production
should become the property of the State, just as the post-
office and the telegraphs have become the property of the
State.

Socialists demand that the State shall manage the railways and the mines and the mills just as it now manages
the post-offices and the telegraphs.

Socialists declare that if it is wicked and foolish and
impossible for the State to manage the factories, mines,
and railways, then it is wicked and foolish and impossible
for the State to manage the telegraphs.

Socialists declare that as the State carries the people's
letters and telegrams more cheaply and more efficiently

than they were carried by private enterprise, so it could grow corn and weave cloth and work the railway systems more cheaply and more efficiently than they are now worked by private enterprise.

Socialists declare that as our Government now makes food and clothing and arms and accoutrements for the army and navy and police, so it could make them for the people.

Socialists declare that as many corporations make gas, provide and manage the water-supply, look after the paving and lighting and cleansing of the streets, and often do a good deal of building and farming, so there is no reason why they should not get coal, and spin yarn, and make boots, and bread, and beer for the people.

Socialists point out that if all the industries of the nation were put under State control, all the profit, which now goes into the hands of a few idle men, would go into the coffers of the State—which means that the people would enjoy the benefits of all the wealth they create.

This, then, is the basis of Socialism, that England should be owned by the English, and managed for the benefit of the English, instead of being owned by a few rich idlers, and mismanaged by them for the benefit of themselves.

But Socialism means more than the mere transference of the wealth of the nation to the nation.

Socialism would not endure competition. Where it found two factories engaged in under-cutting each other at the price of long hours and low wages to the workers, it would step in and fuse the two concerns into one, save an immense sum in cost of working, and finally produce more goods and better goods at a lower figure than were produced before.

But Practical Socialism would do more than that. It would educate the people. It would provide cheap and pure food. It would extend and elevate the means of study and amusement. It would foster literature and science and art. It would encourage and reward genius and industry. It would abolish sweating and jerry work. It would demolish the slums and erect good and handsome dwellings. It would compel all men to do some kind of useful work. It would recreate and nourish the craftsman's pride in his craft. It would protect women and children. It would raise the standard of health and morality; and it would take the sting out of pauperism by paying pensions to honest workers no longer able to work.

Why nationalise the land and instruments of production? To save waste; to save panics; to avert trade depressions, famines, strikes, and congestion of industrial centres; and to prevent greedy and unscrupulous sharpers from enriching themselves at the cost of the national health and prosperity. In short, to replace anarchy and war by law and order. To keep the wolves out of the fold, to tend and fertilise the field of labour instead of allowing the wheat to be strangled by the tares, and to regulate wisely the distribution of the seed-corn of industry so that it might no longer be scattered broadcast— some falling on rocks, and some being eaten up by the birds of the air.

— Reading No. 22 —

SOCIALISTS ON THE ROYAL COMMISSION ON LABOUR, 1894 [22]

Several members of the Royal Commission on Labour were Socialists. They disagreed basically with the conclusions of the majority of their colleagues, and without their knowledge they submitted a minority report which

[22] "Fifth and Final Report of the Royal Commission on Labour, Part I," *Parliamentary Papers*, 1894, XXXV, 146-47.

denounced the capitalist system and supported the public ownership of the means of production.

      *   *   *

To sum up; we regard the unsatisfactory relations between employers and employed as but one inevitable incident of the present industrial anarchy. The only complete solution of the problem is, in our opinion, to be found in the progress of the industrial evolution, which will assign to the "captains of industry," as well as to the manual workers, their proper position as servants of the community.

Meanwhile, the relations between capitalists and manual workers are enormously embittered by the demoralising conditions in which great masses of the population are compelled to live. Under any conceivable view of social development, these conditions demand the serious attention of the Government, and constitute, in our opinion, the most pressing of all the problems of statesmanship.

The evil influences of the "sweated trades," the demoralising irregularity of employment, the insanitary condition, both of the workplaces and the homes, of large sections of the community, the inadequate wages obtained in all the less skilled grades of workers, the excessive hours of labour which prevail throughout so large a part of the industrial field, all call for immediate action.

We think it high time that the whole strength and influence of the collective organisation of the community should be deliberately, patiently, and persistently used to raise the standard of life of its weaker and most oppressed members. We regard this as one of the primary functions of democratic Government, whether national or local, and whilst leaving on one side as beyond our scope such fundamental matters as the nationalisation of the land, and the taxation of unearned incomes, we have suggested, in some detail, various immediately practicable reforms in this direction. These reforms include:—

(a) The explicit and widely advertised adoption by the Government and all local authorities, of direct public employment whenever this is advantageous, the Eight Hours' Day, Trade Union conditions, and a moral minimum wage.

(b) The extension of the factory and similar Acts to all manual workers in all trades, and their drastic enforcement in such a way as to discourage home-work, and absolutely prevent industrial oppression.

(c) The securing by appropriate law of an Eight Hours' Day for every manual worker.

(d) The thorough investigation and bold experimental treatment of the problem of the unemployed.

(e) The provision of adequate sanitary housing accommodation for the whole nation; as well as honourable maintenance for all its workers in their old age.

In short, the whole force of democratic statesmanship must, in our opinion, henceforth be directed to the substitution, as fast as possible, of public for capitalist enterprise, and where this substitution is not yet practicable, to the strict and detailed regulation of all industrial operations, so as to secure to every worker the conditions of efficient citizenship.

MICHAEL DAVITT AND THE LAND LEAGUE, 1882[23]

Michael Davitt's Land League was a response to the agricultural depression that struck Ireland in the 1870's. Although the leaders of the League differed widely in their views of agrarian reform, they agreed that the old system of landlord-tenant relationships had to be abandoned. What made them so formidable a force was the widespread support they won from a peasantry that hated landlordism.

✓ ✓ ✓

It has ever been, and is still, the fate of English Ministers never to know how to remedy any of our admitted wrongs by what are termed "instalments of justice" in a politic or conciliatory manner. Our people must be driven either to open attempts at rebellion, or Ireland be plunged into a ferment of political agitation, ere British statesmanship will admit that such wrongs, or the questions that embrace them, come within the domain of practical politics. But that is not all. Before these recognised grievances can be partially or wholly redressed, or a modicum of justice conceded, the Habeas Corpus Act must be suspended in order that Dublin Castle may be propitiated by an equivalent instalment of political vengeance. Thus the credit which could be gained from a not ungrateful people by a judicious treatment of the social and political wants of our country is lost to England through the vindictive spirit by which her concessions are accompanied to a sensitive and impulsive nation.

The concession upon the Arrears question is now

[23] Michael Davitt, *The Land League Proposal: A Statement for Honest and Thoughtful Men* (Glasgow, 1882), pp. 11-15.

offered side by side with a bill purporting to be aimed at
secret societies and for the prevention of crime—(*loud
hisses*)—but in reality intended to arrest the further
public action of the people of Ireland towards the aboli-
tion of landlordism. Here, in the face of the most
propitious hour that has presented itself to English statesmanship during the past eighty years for an effective
settlement of the Irish difficulty, the fatal dual policy of
the past is again resorted to, and outrage upon liberty,
personal and political, is flung like a brand into Ireland,
to excite again the angry passions which lead to lawless-
ness and crime. I am confident that if the healthy feeling
of horror which was created throughout Ireland by the
Phoenix Park tragedy was permitted to have its full effect
upon the popular mind of the country, assassination
would have been assassinated in Ireland by the melancholy event of the 6th of May. Now the country will see
the use that Mr. Gladstone is about to make of that
event. (*A voice: "No."*) The Land League movement is
to be crushed. (*Cries of "Never," and cheers.*) Every
barrier that could stand between the people and landlord
vengeance is to be removed in order that no political
action in Ireland shall interfere with the subtle policy of
the Whig Government in support of a doomed system.

What will be the consequence? The people of Ireland
can never place confidence in any English Government
—(*hear, hear*)—that places the administration of its laws
in the hands of Dublin Castle—(*hear, hear*)—that depôt
of centralised despotism—(*loud cheers*)—without a
parallel in the history of constitutional government. Those
in whom they have reposed confidence, to whom they
look for guidance and support, are menaced with gagging
laws, the very discussion of which in the English House
of Commons has brought shame to the face of thousands
of Englishmen.

What will be the consequence? The field of Irish political strife will be left clear to the landlords, armed with
unlimited power by Mr. Gladstone, and the equally
unlimited power of secret combination, freed from the
antagonism and rivalry of an open movement. To which
of these two powers will the victims of Irish landlordism
—those who know the implacable nature of landlord

vengeance so well—secretly incline? I will answer this question in memorable words once uttered by John Bright: "When law refuses its duty, when Government denies the right of a people, when competition is so fierce for the little land which the monopolists grant to cultivation in Ireland, when, in fact, for a bare potato millions are scrambling, these people are driven back from law and the usages of civilisation to that which is termed the law of nature, and if not the strongest, the law of the vindictive; and in this case the people of Ireland believe, to my certain knowledge, that it is only by these acts of vengeance, periodically committed, that they can hold in suspense the arm of the proprietor and the agent—(*hear, hear*)—who, in too many cases, if he dared, would exterminate them.

"At this moment there is a state of war in Ireland. Don't let us disguise it from ourselves. There is a war between landlord and tenant; a war as fierce, as relentless, as though it were carried on by force of arms. There is a suspicion, too, between landlord and tenant, which is not known between any class of people in this country, and there is a hatred, too, which I believe, under the present and past system, has been pursued in Ireland, which can never be healed or eradicated." These expressions of John Bright's, years ago, face to face with a similar state of affairs in Ireland as that which confronts us now, I bring forward to show to Mr. Gladstone and the English people what will be the consequences of this battle of vengeance that is going to commence between the landlords of Ireland and a great portion of the people of Ireland. In presence of this state of affairs in Ireland, vengeance is to be pitted against vengeance, the settlement of the agrarian war is to be left between the Clifford Lloyds—(*loud hooting*)—and the wild justice of revenge born of landlord oppression.

I again ask, what will be the consequence? Had Mr. Gladstone been in the confidence of the secret powers with which he pretends alone to grapple he could not have more completely played into their hands. It is only when a people despair of justice at the hands of their rulers, and see their hereditary enemies unopposed by any protective movement, that occult agencies are looked upon with favour by such people, and that the sympathies of the injured are extended to those who avenge the wrongs that are inflicted in the name of law. There is no power at the disposal of Mr. Gladstone, there is no method short of the extermination of the whole Irish race, that can grapple effectually with a secret movement when it is made to appear as the only protector of a wronged and trampled people—(*loud cheers*)—and which confronts the mandates of unlimited despotism with the weapon of retaliation.

If the Land League is to be prevented from succouring the evicted, if every channel of political effort not favourable to Whig legislation on the land question is to be closed up, then, indeed, will the whole situation be surrendered to the secret movement, and *lex talionis* become the only refuge of despair. As the moral responsibility of the outrage epidemic of the past twelve months must, in my humble opinion, rest upon the Whig Administration for its coercive incitation to vengeance, so must the crimes that will follow additional coercion be placed at the same door. If Mr. Gladstone is earnest in his efforts to put down crime, let him go to the source of all agrarian outrage, and remove Irish landlordism from Ireland. (*Cheers.*) If he be determined to put down secret societies, let him remove from the government of Ireland what makes English rule detested and English law distrusted—let him sweep away Dublin Castle—(*loud cheers*)—and show that he can repose the same confidence in Ireland that has not been abused in Canada. (*Cheers.*) If he believes that peace will be restored in Ireland while landlords have power to evict and the Castle power to trample upon every political opponent and every vestige of liberty, he has read the history of the Anglo-Irish difficulty to no purpose. As well might the doctor dream of restoring to health and vigour a patient in whose sensitive flesh the instrument that made the wound lies unremoved.

I believe the admirable temper and manly self-control that has distinguished almost the whole of this country during the past fortnight, in face of what might have provoked an outburst of unjust and ungenerous wrath, together with the wide-spread anxiety that peace should

be restored to Ireland and crime extinguished by generous and just legislation, would sanction measures of justice
and conciliation which the past would not contemplate,
and which the future, if embittered by angry passions and
violence, may refuse to consider. Has Mr. Gladstone the
courage to respond to this feeling among the unprejudiced
of his countrymen, and to make an heroic concession to
justice and right; or will he continue, as in the new Coercion Bill, to be guided by the policy of a Forster—
(*loud hisses*)—and the tactics of political adversaries? It
would be vain for me to think that he would be guided
in his actions by a man like myself. But humble and obscure though my origin and position may be—(*prolonged
cheers*)—the son of an Irish peasant—(*cheers*)—who
was refused shelter in an Irish workhouse by Irish landlordism; the son of an Irish mother who had to beg
through the streets of England for bread for me—humble
as that origin may be, the memory of that mother has
made me swear that so long as I have tongue to speak,
or head to plan, or hand to dare for Ireland—(*cheers,
during which a great part of the audience rose and applauded vociferously*)—Irish landlordism and English
misgovernment in Ireland shall find in me a sleepless
and incessant opponent. (*Renewed cheers.*)

It is useless to think that Mr. Gladstone would be influenced by my advice, but had my voice been listened to
when I last emerged from the prison into which his
Government thrust me in 1870—(*shame*)—the sad history of the past two years would never have to be written,
and the Ireland of to-day might have been otherwise
than a standing reproach to English government. I tell
him now, that, although the Arrears Bill may land his
Government over a temporary difficulty, the very next
season of scarcity or partial famine that unpropitious
seasons will bring upon Ireland, will re-open the Irish
Land question, and call into play the same passions and
provoke the same strife between conflicting interests that
have brought the Land League into existence and forced
the hands of unwilling legislation. If he persists in dealing
only with the Irish social problem as intensified by the
Land League agitation, instead of grappling with it as
Irish Land reformers propose in connection with a train

of retrospective ruin, present discontent, and the certainty of landlordism continuing to move in a circle of reproductive wrong, he will bequeath the settlement of the Irish Land war to the future, and leave the primary cause of Irish poverty, disaffection, crime, and misery to the country he is anxious should look to him as its friend.

Dark as is the present outlook for Ireland, I do not despair. (*Hear, hear.*) In a period of unexampled trial, the attitude of her people has been steadfast, courageous, and unbroken. The march of the social has dragged the settlement of the national question in its wake. If victory has not yet crowned the efforts of the Land League, we have called into existence the elements of proximate success. (*Cheers.*) From every prison in Ireland voices will go forth to teach the oft-repeated lesson that force is no remedy—(*cheers*)—against a cause which rests for support and sanction upon the ordinances of God and the dictates of justice and reason. Every parish in Ireland will have one or more in its midst that has suffered in the cause of liberty and fatherland; and from this outcrop of national sentiment, from men unjustly punished, women imprisoned—(*shame*)—and children indoctrinated in the creed of patriotism and social rights, will spring a generation before whose might no wrong can stand, and from whose birthland every vestige of social and political servitude must fall, as fall the withered leaves of autumn before the angry blasts of winter. (*Cheers.*)

— Reading No. 24 —

LIBERAL CONVERTS TO HOME RULE [24]

Since the agricultural depression made it impossible for many Irish tenants to pay their rent, evictions became a commonplace. To stop these evictions, tenants threatened and attacked landlords and their agents. The spread of violence in Ireland shocked Englishmen, some of whom came to believe that since England could not maintain order in Ireland, the only solution was to let the Irish rule themselves. Among the intellectual leaders of these Liberal converts to home rule was James Bryce.

✓   ✓   ✓

Very few words are needed to summarize the outline which, omitting many details which would have illustrated and confirmed its truth, I have attempted to present of the progress of opinion among Liberal members of the Parliament of 1880.

1. Our experience of the Coercion Bills of 1881 and 1882 disclosed the enormous mischief which such measures do in alienating the minds of Irishmen, and the difficulty of enlisting Irish sentiment on behalf of the law. The results of the Act of 1881 taught us that the repression of open agitation means the growth of far more dangerous conspiracy; those of the Act of 1882 proved that even under an administration like Lord Spencer's repression works no change for the better in the habits and ideas of the people.

2. The conduct of the House of Lords in 1880 and 1881, and the malign influence which its existence exerted whenever remedial legislation for Ireland came in ques-

[24] James Bryce, "How We Became Home Rulers," in James Bryce, ed., *Handbook of Home Rule, Being Articles on the Irish Question* (2nd ed., London, 1887), pp. 51-54.

tion, convinced us that full and complete justice will never be done to Ireland by the British Parliament while the Upper House (as at present constituted) remains a part of that Parliament.

3. The break-down of the procedure of the House of Commons, and the failure of the efforts to amend it, proved that Parliament cannot work so long as a considerable section of its members seek to impede its working. To enable it to do its duty by England and Scotland, it was evidently necessary, either to make the Irish members as loyal to Parliament as English and Scotch members usually are, or else to exclude them.

4. The discussions of Irish Bills in the House of Commons made us realize how little English members knew about Ireland; how utterly different were their competence for, and their attitude towards, Irish questions and English questions. We perceived that we were legislating in the dark for a country whose economic and social condition we did not understand—a country to which we could not apply our English ideas of policy; a country whose very temper and feeling were strange to us. We were really fitter to pass laws for Canada or Australia than for this isle within sight of our shores.

5. I have said that we were legislating in the dark. But there were two quarters from which light was proffered, the Irish members and the Irish Executive. We rejected the first, and could hardly help doing so, for to accept it would have been to displace our own leaders. We followed the light which the Executive gave. But in some cases (as notably in the case of the Coercion Bill of 1881) it proved to be a "wandering fire," leading us into dangerous morasses. And we perceived that at all times legislation at the bidding of the Executive, against the wishes of Irish members, was not self-government or free government. It was despotism. The rule of Ireland by the British Parliament was really "the rule of a dependency through an official, responsible no doubt, but responsible not to the ruled, but to an assembly of which they form less than a sixth part." As this assembly closed its ears to the one-sixth, and gave effect to the will of the official, this was essentially arbitrary government, and wanted those elements of success which free government contains.

This experience had, by 1884, convinced us that the present relations of the British Parliament to Ireland were bad, and could not last; that the discontent of Ireland was justified; that the existing system, in alienating the mind of Ireland, tended, not merely to Repeal, but to Separation; that the simplest, and probably the only effective, remedy for the increasing dangers was the grant of an Irish Legislature. Two events clinched these conclusions. One was the Tory surrender of June, 1885. Self-government, we had come to see, was the only alternative to Coercion, and now Coercion was gone. The other was the General Election of December, 1885, when newly-enfranchised Ireland, through five-sixths of her representatives, demanded a Parliament of her own.

These were not, as is sometimes alleged, conclusions of despair. We were mostly persons of a cautious and conservative turn of mind, as men imbued with the spirit of the British Constitution ought to be. The first thing was to convince us that the existing relations of the islands were faulty, and could not be maintained. This was a negative result, and while we remained in that stage we were despondent. Many Liberal members will remember the gloom that fell on us in 1882 and 1883 whenever we thought or spoke of Ireland. But presently the clouds lifted. We still felt the old objections to any Home Rule scheme, though we now saw that they were less formidable than the evils of the present system. But we came to feel that the grant of self-government was a right thing in itself. It was not merely a means of ridding ourselves of our difficulties, not merely a boon yielded because long demanded. It was a return to broad and deep principles, a conformity to those natural laws which govern human society as well as the inanimate world—an effort to enlist the better and higher feelings of mankind in the creation of a truer union between the two nations than had ever yet existed. When we perceived this, hope returned. It is strong with us now, for, though we see troubles, perhaps even dangers, in the immediate future, we are confident that the principles on which Liberal policy towards Ireland is based will in the long run work out a happy issue for her, as they have in and for every other country that has trusted to them.

One last word as to Consistency. We learnt in the Parliament of 1880 many facts about Ireland we had not
known before; we felt the force and bearing of other facts
previously accepted on hearsay, but not realized. We saw
the Irish problem change from what it had been in 1880
into the new phase which stood apparent at the end of
1885, Coercion abandoned by its former advocates, Self-
government demanded by the nation. Were we to disre-
gard all these new facts, ignore all these new conditions,
and cling to old ideas, some of which we perceived to be
mistaken, while others, still true in themselves, were out-
weighed by arguments of far wider import? We did not so
estimate our duty. We foresaw the taunts of foes and the
reproaches of friends. But we resolved to give effect to the
opinions we slowly, painfully, even reluctantly formed,
opinions all the stronger because not suddenly adopted,
and founded upon evidence whose strength no one can
appreciate till he has studied the causes of Irish discontent
in Irish history, and been forced (as we were) to face in
Parliament the practical difficulties of the government of
Ireland by the British House of Commons.

— Reading No. 25 —

MATTHEW ARNOLD AND IRISH ANARCHY, 1886 [25]

While Irish violence convinced some Englishmen of the
desirability of Irish home rule, it convinced others of its

[25] George W. E. Russell, ed., *Letters of Matthew Arnold,
1848-1888* (London, 1895), II, 384-85, 388, 390-91,
395-96.

impossibility: people who had recourse to crime could not be trusted to govern themselves. Among the leaders of the resistance to home rule Matthew Arnold figured prominently. He was in the United States when the home rule bill of 1886 was being debated, and his reactions to American views of the Irish problem were typical of those of many of his contemporaries.

✓   ✓   ✓

Germantown, June 9, 1886

. . . The cable is the only quick correspondent; owing to the difference of time they were able to cry the House of Commons division in the New York streets on Monday night. And the papers have long accounts of what passed —all coloured by favour to the Irish, but still very interesting. They had made up their minds here that Gladstone was going to win; from the first I had thought he would lose, but I was not prepared for so good a majority. A load is taken off my spirit, but unless Lord Hartington and Goschen bestir themselves and seize the occasion, it will pass from them, and the Home Rulers, pure and simple, will win. Of course I have not seen the comments of the English papers on my letter to the *Times,* but on this side the water it has done good by drawing the distinction between giving to the Irish legislative control over their own local affairs, and giving to them a *single national legislative body* to exercise such control. They all here go off saying, "Of course Ireland ought to have Home Rule just as all our States have," and till the thing is pressed on their attention they do not see the difference between what their States have and what Gladstone proposes to do. But this would lead me too far. . . .

Metropolitan Club, Washington,
June 13, 1886.

. . . In this country it is supposed that England refuses every kind of Home Rule, and as this is eminently the country of local government, almost every one goes for Gladstone as the only propounder of a scheme of local government. The moment any politician produces a counter-scheme, free from the great danger of Gladstone's, the separate national Parliament, but giving real

powers of local government, opinion here, which is extremely important if for no other reason than that most
of Parnell's friends come from America, will undergo a
change. The Americans are not really indisposed to England, I believe, but they are not closely informed on Irish
matters, and they see no Home Rule proposed but Gladstone's measure. I doubt if Salisbury is disposed, or Hartington laborious enough, to make one; William and
Goschen together would have been invaluable for this
purpose. . . .

Stockbridge, Mass.
July 8, 1886.

. . . The Americans are fairly puzzled; they thought Parnell was going to win. You cannot make them understand
that his cause is not that of the local self-government
which is universal here and works well. The truth is we
have not their local self-government in England or Scotland any more than in Ireland. Parliament has been at the
same time local and national legislature for these countries, as well as for Ireland. But as government in England
and Scotland has been in accordance with the wishes of
the majority in the respective countries, the system has
worked well enough hitherto, though public business is
now getting too great for it. But in Ireland, where government has been conducted in accordance with the
wishes of the minority and of the British Philistine, the
defects of the system have come into full view. Therefore,
I am most anxious that the question of local government
should be in every one's mind. If it comes to be fairly
discussed, the Americans will be capable of seeing that
there is no more need for merging Ulster in Southern
Ireland than for merging Massachusetts in New York
State. . . .

Stockbridge, Massachusetts,
July 29, 1886.

. . . The Elections are a great relief. What a power of
solid political sense there is in the English nation still!
And now, unless the Conservatives let things drift and
miss their opportunity, we have a really interesting and
fruitful political work before us—the establishment of a
thorough system of local government. How different from

the Wife's Sister, Church Rate and Disestablishment business familiar to modern Liberalism! I thought (and said in the *Times* six weeks before the election) that Gladstone would be beaten, but the majority against him exceeds my best hopes. Then I came here, where the newspapers are all Parnellite and Gladstonian, suffering nothing to appear but what favours the side they are on. They now console themselves (like John Morley) by saying that in six months Gladstone will be in again, and carrying his measure triumphantly. . . .

— Reading No. 26 —

J. A. FROUDE ON THE ECONOMICS OF EMPIRE, 1886[26]

The great depression affected England's relations not only with Ireland but with her empire. Falling prices and profits encouraged a renewal of interest in the economic possibilities of imperialism, and scores of publicists sought to heighten this interest. Outstanding among them was the vigorous and tough-minded historian, James Anthony Froude, who even before the coming of the depression had proclaimed the blessings of empire and who preached them all the more in the age of the depression.

✓   ✓   ✓

The situation has been extremely difficult. It cannot be wondered at, that when war followed on war in New Zea-

[26] James Anthony Froude, *Oceana or England and Her Colonies* (London, 1886), pp. 5-8, 12-14.

land and South Africa, and British money was spent, and
British troops were employed in killing Maoris and Caf-
fres who had done us no harm, and whose crime was believed by many of us to be no more than the possession
of land which others coveted, public opinion at home
grew impatient. Long bills for these wars appeared in the
Budgets year after year. Political economists began to ask
what was the use of colonies which contributed nothing to
the Imperial exchequer, while they were a constant expense to the taxpayer. They had possessed a value once
as a market for English productions, but after the establishment of free trade the world was our market. The
colonies, as part of the world, would still buy of us, and
would continue to do so, whether as British dependencies
or as free. In case of war we should be obliged to defend
them and to scatter our force in doing it. They gave us
nothing. They cost us much. They were a mere ornament,
a useless responsibility: we did not pause to consider
whether, even if it were true that the colonies were at
present a burden to us, we were entitled to cut men of our
own blood and race thus adrift after having encouraged
them to form settlements under our flag. Both parties in
the State had been irritated in turn by their experience in
Downing Street, and for once both were agreed. The
troops were withdrawn from Canada, from Australia,
from New Zealand. A single regiment only was to have
been left at the Cape to protect our naval station. The
unoccupied lands, properly the inheritance of the collective British nation—whole continents large as a second
United States—were hurriedly abandoned to the local
colonial governments. They were equipped with constitu-
tions modelled after our own, which were to endure as
long as the connection with the mother country was maintained; but they were informed, more or less distinctly,
that they were as birds hatched in a nest whose parents
would be charged with them only till they could provide
for themselves, and the sooner they were ready for complete independence, the better the mother country would
be pleased.

This was the colonial policy avowed in private by responsible statesmen, and half-confessed in public fifteen
years ago. And thus it seemed that the second group of

territorial acquisitions which English enterprise had secured was to follow the first. The American provinces had
been lost by invasion of their rights. The rest were to be
thrown away as valueless. The separation might be called
friendly, but the tone which we assumed was as offensive
to the colonists as the intended action was unwelcome,
and if they were obliged to leave us it would not be as
friends that we should part. The English people too had
not been treated fairly. A policy so far-reaching ought to
have been fully explained to them, and not ventured on
without their full consent. A frank avowal of an intention
to shake the colonies off would have been fatal to the
ministry that made it. Ambiguous expressions were explained away when challenged. We were told that self-
government had been given to the colonies only to attach
them to us more completely, while measures were taken
and language was used which were indisputably designed
to lead to certain and early disintegration.

The intention was an open secret among all leading
statesmen, if it can be called a secret at all, and in the
high political circles the result was regarded as assured.
'It is no use,' said an eminent Colonial Office secretary to
myself when I once remonstrated, 'to speak about it any
longer. The thing is done. The great colonies are gone. It
is but a question of a year or two.'

Those were the days of progress by leaps and bounds,
of 'unexampled prosperity,' of the apparently boundless
future which the repeal of the Corn Laws had opened
upon British industry and trade. The fate of Great Britain
was that it was to become the world's great workshop.
Her people were to be kept at home and multiply. With
cheap labour and cheap coal we could defy competition,
and golden streams would flow down in ever-gathering
volumes over landowners and millowners and shipowners.
. . . The 'hands' and the 'hands' ' wives and children? Oh
yes, they too would do very well: wages would rise, food
would be cheap, employment constant. The colonies
brought us nothing. The empire brought us nothing, save
expense for armaments and possibilities of foreign com-
plications. Shorn of these wild shoots we should be like
an orchard tree pruned of its luxuriance, on which the
fruit would grow richer and more abundant. . . .

Our people stream away from us. Out of the hundreds of thousands of English, Scots, and Irish who annually leave our shores, eighty per cent. have gone hitherto to the United States, and only the remaining fraction to the countries over which our own flag is flying. I once asked the greatest, or at least the most famous, of modern English statesmen whether, in the event of a great naval war, we might not look for help to the 60,000 Canadian seamen and fishermen. 'The Canadian seamen,' he said, 'belong to Canada, not to us;' and then going to the distribution of our emigrants, he insisted that there was not a single point in which an Englishman settling in Canada or Australia was of more advantage to us than as a citizen of the American Union. The use of him was as a purchaser of English manufactures—that was all. Sir Arthur Helps told me a story singularly illustrative of the importance which the British official mind has hitherto allowed to the distant scions of Oceana. A Government had gone out; Lord Palmerston was forming a new ministry, and in a preliminary council was arranging the composition of it. He had filled up the other places. He was at a loss for a Colonial Secretary. This name and that was suggested, and thrown aside. At last he said, 'I suppose I must take the thing myself. Come upstairs with me, Helps, when the council is over. We will look at the maps and you shall show me where these places are.'

The temper represented in this cool indifference is passing away. The returns of trade show in the first place that commerce follows the flag. Our colonists take three times as much of our productions in proportion to their numbers as foreigners take. The difference increases rather than diminishes, and the Australian, as a mere consumer, *is* more valuable to us than the American. What more he may be, his voluntary presence at Suakin has indicated for him to all the world. But more than this. It has become doubtful even to the political economist whether England can trust entirely to free trade and competition to keep the place which she has hitherto held. Other nations press us with their rivalries. Expenses increase, manufactures languish or cease to profit. Revenue, once so expansive, becomes stationary. 'Business' may, probably will, blaze up again, but the growth of it can no longer be regarded as constant, while population increases and hungry stomachs multiply, requiring the three meals a day whatever the condition of the markets. Hence those among us who have disbelieved all along that a great nation can venture its whole fortunes safely on the power of underselling its neighbours in calicoes and iron-work no longer address a public opinion entirely cold. It begins to be admitted that were Canada and South Africa and Australia and New Zealand members of one body with us, with a free flow of our population into them, we might sit secure against shifts and changes. In the multiplying number of our own fellow-citizens animated by a common spirit, we should have purchasers for our goods from whom we should fear no rivalry; we should turn in upon them the tide of our emigrants which now flows away, while the emigrants themselves would thrive under their own fig tree, and rear children with stout limbs and colour in their cheeks, and a chance before them of a human existence. Oceana would then rest on sure foundations; and her navy—the hand of her strength and the symbol of her unity—would ride securely in self-supporting stations in the four quarters of the globe.

— Reading No. 27 —

JOSEPH CHAMBERLAIN AND IMPERIAL COÖPERATION, 1897 [27]

Joseph Chamberlain's view of imperialism was profoundly influenced by the great depression. Concerned

[27] "Trade of the British Empire and Foreign Competition," *Parliamentary Papers*, 1897, LX, 16-17.

over foreign competition, falling profits, and unemployment, he saw in the consolidation and expansion of the empire the way out of the depression. One of his first steps as Colonial Secretary was to investigate the extent and nature of foreign competition in British imperial markets.

✓   ✓   ✓

Downing Street, November 28, 1895.

My Lord,
Sir,

I am impressed with the extreme importance of securing as large a share as possible of the mutual trade of the United Kingdom and the Colonies for British producers and manufacturers, whether located in the Colonies or in the United Kingdom.

2. In the first place, therefore, I wish to investigate thoroughly the extent to which in each of the Colonies foreign imports of any kind have displaced, or are displacing, similar British goods and the causes of such displacement.

3. With this object, I take this opportunity of inviting the assistance of your Government in obtaining a return which will show for the years 1884, 1889, and 1894—

(*a.*) The value (if any) of all articles, specified in the classification annexed, imported into the Colony under your Government from any foreign country or countries, whenever (and only when) the value of any article so imported from any foreign country, or countries, was 5 per cent. or upwards of the total value of that article imported into the Colony from all sources, whether within or without the British Empire, and when the total value of that article imported was not less than £500.

(*b.*) The reasons which may have in each case induced the colonial importer to prefer a foreign article to similar goods of British manufacture.

4. These reasons (which should take the shape of a report on each article, separately, of which the foreign import exceeded 5 per cent. of the whole import and of which the total value imported was not less than £500.,

as defined above) should be classified and discussed under one or other of the following heads:—

- (*a.*) Price (delivered in the Colony) of the foreign article as compared with the British. . . .
- (*b.*) Quality and finish, as to which full particulars should be given.
- (*c.*) Suitability of the goods for the market, their style or pattern.

  In connexion with this, and in illustration of the reasons for the displacement of British goods of any class, it is important that patterns or specimens of the goods preferred should be sent home, unless the bulk is very great. This will be necessary chiefly in those cases where the difference cannot be fairly described in writing.
- (*d.*) Difference of making up or packing, as to which full particulars should be given.
- (*e.*) False marking, such as piracy of trade marks, false indications of origin, or false indications of weight, measure, size, or number.
- (*f.*) Any other cause which may exist should, of course, be stated. . . .

9. I shall be glad to have these returns as soon as possible, and shall greatly appreciate your expedition in the matter.

I have the honour to be,
Your most obedient humble Servant,
J. Chamberlain.

TENNYSON AS A POET OF EMPIRE[28]

The growth of interest in imperialism was reflected frequently in the imaginative literature of the late Victorians. Rudyard Kipling rapidly became *the* writer on empire, but he was only one of many men of letters who used literature to defend imperialism. As poet laureate, Tennyson was called upon to write poems celebrating the imperial theme. An ardent believer in empire, he found the task congenial.

HANDS ALL ROUND (1885)

First pledge our Queen this solemn night,
    Then drink to England, every guest;
That man's the true Cosmopolite
    Who loves his native country best.
May freedom's oak for ever live
    With stronger life from day to day;
That man's the best Conservative
    Who lops the moulder'd branch away.
      Hands all round!
    God the traitor's hope confound!
To this great cause of Freedom drink, my friends,
    And the great name of England, round and round.

To all the loyal hearts who long
    To keep our English Empire whole!
To all our noble sons, the strong
    New England of the Southern Pole!
To England under Indian skies,

[28] Alfred, Lord Tennyson, *Tiresias and Other Poems* (London, 1885), pp. 195-97; *Locksley Hall Sixty Years After, Etc.* (London, 1886), pp. 43-45.

To those dark millions of her realm!
To Canada whom we love and prize,
   Whatever statesman hold the helm.
      Hands all round!
   God the traitor's hope confound!
To this great name of England drink, my friends,
   And all her glorious empire, round and round.

To all our statesmen so they be
   True leaders of the land's desire!
To both our Houses, may they see
   Beyond the borough and the shire!
We sail'd wherever ship could sail,
   We founded many a mighty state;
Pray God our greatness may not fail
   Through craven fears of being great.
      Hands all round!
   God the traitor's hope confound!
To this great cause of Freedom drink, my friends,
   And the great name of England, round and round.

OPENING OF THE INDIAN AND COLONIAL EXHIBITION BY THE QUEEN (1886)

I

Welcome, welcome with one voice!
In your welfare we rejoice,
Sons and brothers that have sent,
From isle and cape and continent,
Produce of your field and flood,
Mount and mine, and primal wood;
Works of subtle brain and hand,
And splendours of the morning land,
Gifts from every British zone;
   Britons, hold your own!

II

May we find, as ages run,
The mother featured in the son;
And may yours for ever be
That old strength and constancy
Which has made your fathers great

In our ancient island State,
And wherever her flag fly,
Glorying between sea and sky,
Makes the might of Britain known;
    Britons, hold your own!

III

Britain fought her sons of yore—
Britain fail'd; and never more,
Careless of our growing kin,
Shall we sin our fathers' sin,
Men that in a narrower day—
Unprophetic rulers they—
Drove from out the mother's nest
That young eagle of the West
To forage for herself alone;
    Britons, hold your own!

IV

Sharers of our glorious past,
Brothers, must we part at last?
Shall we not thro' good and ill
Cleave to one another still?
Britain's myriad voices call,
'Sons, be welded each and all,
Into one imperial whole,
One with Britain, heart and soul!
One life, one flag, one fleet, one throne!'
    Britons, hold your own!

SELECT BIBLIOGRAPHY

Baker, Joseph E., ed., *The Reinterpretation of Victorian Literature* (Princeton University Press, Princeton, 1950).

Beer, Max, *A History of British Socialism* (Allen & Unwin, London, Revised Edition, 1940).

Bennett, George, ed., *The Concept of Empire* (Black, London, 1953).

Brinton, Crane, *English Political Thought in the Nineteenth Century* (Benn, London, 1933).

Buckley, Jerome Hamilton, *The Victorian Temper* (Harvard, Cambridge, 1951).

Clapham, Sir John, *An Economic History of Modern Britain*, Vols. II, III (Cambridge, 1932-1938).

Cole, G. D. H., *A Short History of the British Working-Class Movement, 1789-1947* (Allen & Unwin, London, Revised Edition, 1948).

———, *British Working Class Politics, 1832-1914* (Routledge, London, 1941).

Cruse, Amy, *After the Victorians* (Allen & Unwin, London, 1938).

———, *The Victorians and Their Books* (Allen & Unwin, London, 1935).

Dicey, A. V., *Lectures on the Relation between Law and Public Opinion in England during the Nineteenth Century* (Macmillan, London, Revised Edition, 1914).

Elliott-Binns, Leonard, *Religion in the Victorian Era* (Lutterworth, London, 1936).

Ensor, R. C. K., *England, 1870-1914* (Oxford, 1936).

Halévy, Elie, *A History of the English People in the Nineteenth Century*, Vol. V (Benn, London, 1929).

Hammond, J. L., *Gladstone and the Irish Nation* (Longmans, London, 1938).

Hoffman, Ross J. S., *Great Britain and the German Trade Rivalry, 1875-1914* (University of Pennsylvania Press, Philadelphia, 1933).

Howe, Susanne, *Novels of Empire* (Columbia, New York, 1949).

Ideas and Beliefs of the Victorians (Sylvan, London, 1949).

Lynd, Helen M., *England in the Eighteen-Eighties* (Oxford, London, 1945).

Mansergh, Nicholas, *Ireland in the Age of Reform and Revolution* (Allen & Unwin, London, 1940).

Newton, A. P., *A Hundred Years of the British Empire* (Macmillan, New York, 1940).

Park, Joseph H., ed., *British Prime Ministers of the Nineteenth Century* (New York University Press, 1950).

Pelling, Henry, *The Origins of the Labour Party, 1880-1900* (Macmillan, London, 1954).

Reckitt, Maurice B., *Maurice to Temple* (Faber, London, 1947).

Rostow, W. W., *British Economy of the Nineteenth Century* (Oxford, 1948).

Smellie, K. B., *A Hundred Years of English Government* (Duckworth, London, 1937).

Wingfield-Stratford, Esmé, *The Victorian Sunset* (Morrow, New York, 1932).

Young, G. M., *Victorian England, Portrait of an Age* (Oxford, London, 1936).

INDEX

Accident Insurance, 29, 39, 40

Agricultural laborers, 15-17, 100-05

Agriculture, 11-17, 39, 63, 74, 88, 95-105

Anarchists, 66

Anti-Corn Law League, 42

Arch, Joseph, 16, 102-03, 108-11

Aristocracy, 15, 26, 35

Arnold, Matthew, 53, 77, 90, 169-72

Ashbourne Act, 78

Ashton, T. S., 19

Austin, Alfred, 51, 86

Australia, 83, 85, 86

Aveling, Edward, 65

Bagehot, Walter, 17, 48

Beales, H. L., 19

Besant, Mrs. Annie, 56, 68

Besant, Sir Walter, 14, 30, 34

Bismarck, Otto von, 60

Blatchford, Robert, 33, 69-71, 153-57

Board of Agriculture, 14, 39

Boer War, 88, 89

Booth, Charles, 32

Booth, General William, 32, 57-58

Brabazon, Lord, 59

Bradlaugh, Charles, 51, 56, 83

Bright, John, 81, 83

Browning, Robert, 56

Bryce, James, 166-69

Butler, Samuel, 17, 56, 75

Butt, Isaac, 74-75

Canada, 82-83, 85, 86

Carlyle, Thomas, 59, 69

Chamberlain, Joseph, 48, 54-56, 61, 77, 87-88, 113-15, 143-47, 176-78

Child labor, 29, 38-40

Christian Social Union, 62

Church of Ireland, 73

Churchill, Lord Randolph, 19, 48, 51-54, 61, 79, 139-43

Churchill, Sir Winston, 54

Clarion, 69

Cobden, Richard, 81, 83

Coercion Laws, 75-76

Commerce, 18-27, 51, 105-15

Commissioners in Lunacy, 10

Commonweal, 66

Conservative Party, 13, 41, 44-45, 48-54, 56, 83, 88, 135-43

Consular Service, 20, 23-24

Contemporary Review, 44

Corelli, Marie, 20

Cunningham, William, 19

Cyprus, 84

Daily News, 82

Darwinism, 56, 58

Davidson, Thomas, 66

Davitt, Michael, 74-75, 160-65

Derby, Lord, 83

Dickens, Charles, 30

Dilke, Sir Charles Wentworth, 82-83

Disraeli, Benjamin, 13, 30, 38, 48-51, 53, 73-74, 83-84, 135-39

Doyle, Sir Arthur Conan, 20

Education, 17, 24, 26, 29-30, 38, 40

Eight-hour movement, 29, 59
Eliot, George, 30
Ensor, R. C. K., 90-91
Evans, Howard, 100

Fabian Society, 66-69, 151-52
Fair Trade, 27, 108-11
Fellowship of the New Life, 66-67
Fenianism, 72-73
Feudalism, 49
Fiji, 84
France, 13, 85, 88
Free Trade, 13-14, 23, 26
Froude, James Anthony, 85, 172-76

Gaskell, Elizabeth, 30
George, Henry, 12, 69
Germany, 13, 21-27, 60, 81, 85, 87, 88, 112
Giffen, Sir Robert, 29-30, 33
Gilbert, Sir William Schwenck, 20, 38, 40, 72, 78
Gissing, George, 30, 32, 42, 61, 64
Gladstone, Herbert, 76
Gladstone, William Ewart, 38, 39, 51-52, 72-73, 75-80, 81, 84, 91
Green, Thomas Hill, 59
Guild of St. Matthew, 62

Haggard, Sir Henry Rider, 14, 20
Halévy, Elie, 90-91
Hammond, J. L., 76
Harcourt, Sir William, 61
Hardie, Keir, 70-71
Hardy, Thomas, 16, 56, 77
Henley, William Ernest, 86
Home Rule, 56, 74-80, 90, 166-72
Hope, Anthony, 20
Hours of work, 28-29
Housing, 28, 38-39, 50, 54
Humanitarianism, 33-34, 59-60
Huxley, Thomas Henry, 57
Hyndman, Henry Mayers, 63-65

Imperialism, 23, 81-89, 172-81
Independent Labour Party, 70-71
India, 32, 83, 84
Industry, 18-27, 105-15
Irish Question, 72-80, 160-72

Jevons, W. Stanley, 35
Jews, 120
Justice, 64

Kingsley, Charles, 30, 62
Kipling, Rudyard, 32, 57, 86
Kropotkin, Prince, 61

Labour Party, 35, 71-72
Land Acts, 73, 75, 80
Land League, 74-75, 160-65
Lecky, W. E. H., 42
Leeds Chamber of Commerce, 86
Levi, Leone, 30, 115-17
Liberal Party, 41, 44-45, 54-56, 81
Liberal Unionists, 56, 77-78
Liberty and Property Defence League, 41-43, 60, 126-32
Local Government, 40-41
Lockout, 17

McKenzie, Fred A., 21, 25-27
Mallock, William Hurrell, 32, 46-47, 133-35
Malthusianism, 10-11
Manning, Cardinal, 58
Marshall, Alfred, 18
Marx, Eleanor, 65
Marx, Karl, 35-36, 61, 63
Maugham, Somerset, 30
Meredith, George, 56
Mill, John Stuart, 33, 59, 69
Morley, Lord, 61
Morris, William, 31, 63, 64-66, 147-51
Morrison, Arthur, 30

Nesbit, Edith, 67
New Unionism, 34-35

New Zealand, 85
Newspaper press, 43, 59
Nobbe, Susanne Howe, 86

Ouida, 20

Parnell, Charles Stewart, 75-77, 79
Pater, Walter, 65
Paterson, Emma, 34
Pease, Edward R., 68
Plunkett, Sir Horace, 80
Population, 10-11, 80, 82, 85
Poverty, 32-33, 36, 45, 54, 58, 64
Primrose League, 52
Prostitution, 32, 39

Reade, Charles, 30
Religion, 51, 52, 56-59, 62
Republicanism, 83
Rhodes, Cecil, 89
Rogers, Thorold, 19
Rosebery, Lord, 39, 86, 87
Rossetti, Dante Gabriel, 65
Royal Commission on Agriculture, 15-16, 37, 95-100
Royal Commission on Labour, 29, 33-34, 60, 122-26, 157-59
Royal Commission on the Depression of Trade and Industry, 18, 20, 27, 28, 105-08
Ruskin, John, 59, 69, 91
Russia, 50, 85, 88

Salisbury, Lord, 39, 53, 54, 56, 86-87
Salvation Army, 57-58
Seeley, Sir John Robert, 85
Shaw, George Bernard, 32, 59, 62, 67-69
Sherard, Robert, 32
Simmons, Alfred, 104-05
Smiles, Samuel, 71
Smith, Goldwin, 81
Social Democratic Federation, 63-65
Socialism, 25, 35, 41, 47, 51, 60-72, 147-59
Socialist League, 65-66
South Africa, 85, 89

Spencer, Herbert, 43-46, 60, 64
Stead, William T., 59
Stephen, Sir Leslie, 56-57
Stephens, W. Walker, 59
Stevenson, Robert Louis, 20, 86
Strachey, Lytton, 90-91
Strikes, 20, 35
Suez Canal, 84
Sweated workers, 31-32, 117-22
Swinburne, Algernon Charles, 56, 64

Taff Vale Case, 71
Technical education, 20, 23-24, 39, 107
Tennyson, Alfred, Lord, 32, 33-34, 52, 61, 64, 75, 82, 84, 86, 90, 179-81
Times, 19, 49
Toynbee, Arnold, 19
Trade unionism, 16-17, 34-35, 38, 71, 100-05, 122-26
Trusts, 27
Tuckwell, William, 59
Turkey, 84

Uganda, 87
Unemployment, 30-31, 35, 59
United States, 12, 25-27, 81-82, 85, 86, 87, 88
Urbanization, 10-11, 15

Victoria, Queen, 41

Wages, 28-30, 39
Ward, Mrs. Humphry, 57
Webb, Sidney, 40, 62, 68
Wells, H. G., 88
West Africa, 88
Westcott, Brooke, 57
Wilde, Oscar, 15, 24, 39, 53, 60, 63
William II, 88
Williams, Ernest Edwin, 21-25, 111-13
Women workers, 32, 34
Working classes, 28-36, 53, 115-26

Young, G. M., 77, 90-91

Zangwill, Israel, 30

Zola, Emil, 30
Zulus, 84

VAN NOSTRAND ANVIL BOOKS already published

1 *MAKING OF MODERN FRENCH MIND*—Kohn
2 *THE AMERICAN REVOLUTION*—Morris
3 *THE LATE VICTORIANS*—Ausubel
4 *WORLD IN THE 20th CENTURY*—Rev. Ed. Snyder
5 *50 DOCUMENTS OF THE 20th CENTURY*—Snyder
6 *THE AGE OF REASON*—Snyder
7 *MARX AND THE MARXISTS*—Hook
8 *NATIONALISM*—Kohn
9 *MODERN JAPAN*—Rev. Ed. Tiedemann
10 *50 DOCUMENTS OF THE 19th CENTURY*—Snyder
11 *CONSERVATISM*—Viereck
12 *THE PAPACY*—Corbett
13 *AGE OF THE REFORMATION*—Bainton
14 *DOCUMENTS IN AMERICAN HISTORY*—Rev. Ed. Morris
15 *CONTEMPORARY AFRICA*—Rev. Ed. Wallbank
16 *THE RUSSIAN REVOLUTIONS OF 1917*—Curtiss
17 *THE GREEK MIND*—Agard
18 *BRITISH CONSTITUTIONAL HISTORY SINCE 1832*—Schuyler and Weston
19 *THE NEGRO IN THE U.S.*—Logan
20 *AMERICAN CAPITALISM*—Hacker
21 *LIBERALISM*—Schapiro
22 *THE FRENCH REVOLUTION, 1789-1799*—Gershoy
23 *HISTORY OF MODERN GERMANY*—Snyder
24 *HISTORY OF MODERN RUSSIA*—Kohn
25 *NORTH ATLANTIC CIVILIZATION*—Kraus
26 *NATO*—Salvadori
27 *DOCUMENTS IN U.S. FOREIGN POLICY*—Brockway
28 *AMERICAN FARMERS' MOVEMENTS*—Shannon
29 *HISTORIC DECISIONS OF SUPREME COURT*—Swisher
30 *MEDIEVAL TOWN*—Mundy and Riesenberg
31 *REVOLUTION AND REACTION 1848-1852*—Bruun
32 *SOUTHEAST ASIA AND WORLD TODAY*—Buss
33 *HISTORIC DOCUMENTS OF W. W. I*—Snyder
34 *HISTORIC DOCUMENTS OF W. W. II*—Langsam
35 *ROMAN MIND AT WORK*—MacKendrick
36 *SHORT HISTORY OF CANADA*—Masters
37 *WESTWARD MOVEMENT IN U.S.*—Billington
38 *DOCUMENTS IN MEDIEVAL HISTORY*—Downs
39 *HISTORY OF AMERICAN BUSINESS*—Cochran
40 *DOCUMENTS IN CANADIAN HISTORY*—Talman
41 *FOUNDATIONS OF ISRAEL*—Janowsky
42 *MODERN CHINA*—Rowe
43 *BASIC HISTORY OF OLD SOUTH*—Stephenson
44 *THE BENELUX COUNTRIES*—Eyck
45 *MEXICO AND THE CARIBBEAN*—Rev. Ed. Hanke
46 *SOUTH AMERICA*—Rev. Ed. Hanke
47 *SOVIET FOREIGN POLICY, 1917-1941*—Kennan
48 *THE ERA OF REFORM, 1830-1860*—Commager
49 *EARLY CHRISTIANITY*—Bainton
50 *RISE AND FALL OF THE ROMANOVS*—Mazour
51 *CARDINAL DOCUMENTS IN BRITISH HISTORY*—Schuyler and Weston
52 *HABSBURG EMPIRE 1804-1918*—Kohn
53 *CAVOUR AND UNIFICATION OF ITALY*—Salvadori
54 *ERA OF CHARLEMAGNE*—Easton and Wieruszowski
55 *MAJOR DOCUMENTS IN AMERICAN ECONOMIC HISTORY, Vol. I*—Hacker
56 *MAJOR DOCUMENTS IN AMERICAN ECONOMIC HISTORY, Vol. II*—Hacker
57 *HISTORY OF THE CONFEDERACY*—Vandiver
58 *COLD WAR DIPLOMACY*—Graebner
59 *MOVEMENTS OF SOCIAL DISSENT IN MODERN EUROPE*—Schapiro
60 *MEDIEVAL COMMERCE*—Adelson
61 *THE PEOPLE'S REPUBLIC OF CHINA*—Buss
62 *WORLD COMMUNISM*—Hook